Endorseme[
*Welcome to a Refor*

"In the providence of God through Rev. Daniel Hyde, you have in your hands an excellent instrument to use in developing the life and ministry of new members, church leaders, and all disciples. This book illustrates the blessings of the historical legacy of the Reformed church with confessional integrity to equip believers and churches with evangelical breadth and theological depth. This is sound doctrine for sound lives. The key to the apostolic church is prominently displayed and easily accessible throughout the pages of *Welcome to a Reformed Church*."

—*Dr. Harry L. Reeder, III*
Senior pastor, Briarwood Presbyterian Church (PCA)
Birmingham, Alabama

"As one who has made much the same journey as I did, Rev. Hyde offers a thoughtful and compelling guide to the distinctive emphases of the Reformed churches for those coming to them. He explains how those wonderful doctrines are worked out in the life and worship of Reformed and Presbyterian churches. If only I had had a book like Rev. Hyde's *Welcome to a Reformed Church*, my own journey would have been a bit easier, for I would have had someone to 'connect the dots' for me."

—*Dr. Kim Riddlebarger*
Senior pastor, Christ Reformed Church (URCNA)
Anaheim, California

"Daniel Hyde has written an invaluable road map for pilgrims new and old so they can know what Reformed churches believe and why. With this book, Christians can navigate the often-confusing landscape of different denominations and understand what makes Reformed churches unique and, more important, biblical. Pastor Hyde's work is clear, succinct, informative, and faithful to the Scriptures. I highly recommend this work to anyone who desires to understand the theological pillars of the Reformed faith."

—Dr. J. V. Fesko
Academic dean and associate professor of systematic theology
Westminster Seminary California
Escondido, California

"Daniel Hyde's popular introduction to the Reformed faith will prove a wonderful tool for busy pastors who are looking for help in welcoming new believers into membership in the local church. *Welcome to a Reformed Church* will also serve as a kind of road map for those who are new to the Reformed faith—to its history, confessions, doctrinal commitments, and patterns of worship and ministry. In its own way, this book is a great example of the kind of 'hospitality' Reformed churches are called to show to those whom the Lord is gathering into their fellowship by His Spirit and Word."

—Dr. Cornelis Venema
President and professor of doctrinal studies
Mid-America Reformed Seminary
Dyer, Indiana

"As a minister in a Reformed church, I am delighted to be able to commend this book by Daniel Hyde, as it provides one of the most useful studies of the basics of Reformed belief, worship, and practice that I have come across. I will be commending it not only for people wishing to know more about the basics of the Reformed faith, but also for those who sit in Reformed churches and need to know more

service by giving us this well-written, concise, easy-to-understand book explaining what it means to be a 'Reformed' church. Yet, at the same time, this is a theologically deep book that will send us back to Scripture and our confessions so that we might understand just what the church really is. In a day of great doctrinal confusion, especially about the church, I know of no better tool to give to those who want to know more about Reformed churches."

—*Rev. Kevin Efflandt*
Pastor, Bellingham United Reformed Church (URCNA)
Bellingham, Washington

"As a fellow import to the Reformed faith from the Pentecostal/charismatic movement, I can say that Daniel Hyde has summarized our Reformed distinctives in a clear and concise manner, answering many of the questions modern evangelicals ask. I heartily commend this book to newcomers in my church and all Reformed churches."

—*Rev. Jerrold Lewis*
Pastor, Lacombe Free Reformed Church (FRCNA)
Lacombe, Alberta

# A GUIDE FOR PILGRIMS

## DANIEL R. HYDE

Reformation Trust

PUBLISHING

A DIVISION OF LIGONIER MINISTRIES · ORLANDO, FLORIDA

*Welcome to a Reformed Church: A Guide for Pilgrims*

© 2010 by Daniel R. Hyde

Published by Reformation Trust Publishing
a division of Ligonier Ministries
400 Technology Park, Lake Mary, FL 32746
www.ligonier.org    www.reformationtrust.com

Printed in Grand Rapids, Michigan
Color House Graphics
May 2011
First edition, second printing

Cover design: Tobias' Outerwear for Books
Interior design and typeset: Katherine Lloyd, THE DESK

Unless otherwise indicated, all Scripture quotations are from *The Holy Bible, English Standard Version*, copyright © 2001 by Crossway Bibles, a division of Good News Publishers. Used by permission. All rights reserved.

Scripture quotations marked NASB are from *The New American Standard Bible.* Copyright © The Lockman Foundation 1960, 1962, 1963, 1968, 1971, 1972, 1973, 1975, 1995. Used by permission.

Scripture quotations marked NIV are from *The Holy Bible, New International Version*. NIV*. Copyright © 1973, 1978, 1984 by International Bible Society. Used by permission of Zondervan. All rights reserved.

Scripture quotations marked KJV are from *The Holy Bible, King James Version*.

Scripture quotations marked ASV are from *The Holy Bible, American Standard Version*.

Unless otherwise indicated, all quotations of the Christian creeds and Reformed confessions are from *The Creeds of Christendom*, ed. Philip Schaff, rev. David S. Schaff, 3 vols. (repr.; Grand Rapids: Baker, 1996).

**Library of Congress Cataloging-in-Publication Data**

Hyde, Daniel R.
  Welcome to a Reformed Church : a guide for pilgrims / Daniel R. Hyde.
      p. cm.
  Includes bibliographical references (p.      ) and indexes.
  ISBN 978-1-56769-203-7
  1. Reformed Church--Doctrines.  I. Title.
  BX9422.3.H93 2010
  230'.42--dc22
                                                        2009049652

A father in the faith, a friend in the Lord, and a
living example of what it means to be sober-minded,
dignified, and self-controlled, sound in faith,
in love, and in steadfastness (Titus 2:2)

## ABBREVIATIONS

BC—Belgic Confession

Calvin, *Institutes*—John Calvin, *Institutes of the Christian Religion*, ed. John T. McNeill, trans. Ford Lewis Battles, The Library of Christian Classics, Vols. XX–XXI (Philadelphia: The Westminster Press, 1960).

CD—Canons of Dort

HC—Heidelberg Catechism

WCF—Westminster Confession of Faith

WLC—Westminster Larger Catechism

WSC—Westminster Shorter Catechism

g . . . . . young leaves of brilliant green are bursting from once-bare trees. Azaleas, dogwoods, and wisterias lend vivid and dazzling color to what weeks ago was a colorless landscape. I know that spring is coming because there are signs of life all around me.

In the church of Jesus Christ, signs all around are pointing to renewed spiritual life. A younger generation of men and women has embraced Reformed theology in numbers unparalleled in recent memory. Web sites, conferences, publishing houses, and seminaries dedicated to promoting Reformed theology are flourishing. Most important, God is changing lives by the gospel of His grace. He is bringing dead sinners to new life in Jesus Christ, and longtime Christians are experiencing the beauty and glory of the sovereign grace of God in a newfound power and depth. These Christians are flocking to join churches where the "whole counsel of God" (Acts 20:27) is taught without reservation and without compromise.

Perhaps you were raised in a Reformed church or have recently joined a Reformed church. You want to know more about why your church believes what it believes and lives the way that it lives. Or perhaps you are a curious outsider. You have been hearing a lot about Reformed theology and the Reformed church, and you want to learn more.

Wherever you are, you may be asking questions: What do Reformed churches believe? What do they have to say about how I should live my Christian life? Why do they worship the way they do? Why is their worship different from some other churches in my community?

We can answer these questions by asking and answering three interlocking questions: What do Reformed churches believe? How do Reformed churches live? How do Reformed churches worship?

## WHAT DO REFORMED CHURCHES BELIEVE?

It is tempting to answer this question by trying to figure out what well-known and contemporary Reformed teachers, pastors, and professors believe the Bible to teach, but Reformed churches have a more accessible and objective way to answer this question, namely, the church's creeds and confessions.

The sole foundation of every creed and confession adopted by Reformed churches is the Bible. Because we believe that the Bible is the inspired, inerrant Word of God, the only rule of faith and obedience, we therefore confess only what we find expressly taught in the text of Scripture or what we can necessarily infer from the teaching of Scripture.

Some creeds and confessions are unique to Reformed churches. These include the Three Forms of Unity (the Belgic Confession, the Heidelberg Catechism, and the Canons of Dort) and the Westminster Standards (the Westminster Confession of Faith and the Westminster Larger and Shorter catechisms). As Rev. Daniel R. Hyde points out in this book, other creeds and confessions are shared with the church at large. We confess with the broader church the truths found in the Apostles', Nicene-Constantinopolitan, and Athanasian creeds. We have not broken from but are part of the catholic, or universal, church. We say, with the nineteenth-century Scottish Presbyterian theologian John "Rabbi" Duncan (1796–1870), "I'm first, Christ

...... Protestants are the true catholics. Such Protestants endeavor to hold fast to the pattern of sound words that Christ, the only King and Head of the church, has given to the whole church through His apostles (2 Tim. 1:13). Rome has departed in fundamental ways from this pattern. The claim to catholicity, these Protestants maintain, is valid only when it is attached to the reality of apostolicity. It is in this sense that Reformed churches are truly catholic. The great doctrines that shook the church at the time of the Protestant Reformation and have come to define classical Protestantism—Scripture alone and justification by faith alone—are catholic doctrines because they are biblical doctrines.

## HOW DO REFORMED CHURCHES LIVE?

Reformed churches prize sound doctrine. They aim to reflect the depth and penetration of biblical teaching in their pulpits. Sound doctrine, however, is never an end in itself. We affirm, with the apostle Paul, that truth "accords with godliness" (Titus 1:1; 1 Tim. 6:3). The early English Puritan William Ames (1576–1633) put it well when, in beginning his classic theology textbook *The Marrow of Theology,* he stated, "Theology is the doctrine or teaching of living to God."[2]

God has established an inseparable connection between truth and godliness. If truth remains in our heads but does not proceed to dwell in our hearts and find expression in our conduct, then we are no different, James says, than the devils (James 2:18–19). On the other hand, we cannot expect to grow in authentic godliness unless we are at the same time growing in our grasp of biblical truth (John 17:17; 2 Thess. 2:13; 2 Peter 3:18; Pss. 37:31; 119:11). Pursuing godliness without also pursuing biblical truth is a sure-fire way to remain in spiritual infancy (Eph. 4:14). The fruit of a life uninformed by serious biblical content sadly mars the modern American religious landscape: faddishness, emotional manipulation, and the confusion of personal feelings and impulses with authentic spiritual direction.

This is why the life of Reformed churches is directed exclusively by the Bible—its study, reading, preaching, meditation, memorization, and application across the spectrum of life. The Bible guides and leads us by pointing us to the source, standard, and goal of all Christian living.

The source of all Christian living is the union of the believer with Jesus Christ. Inseparably united by the Holy Spirit to Christ in His death and resurrection, we are therefore dead to sin and alive to God in righteousness (see Rom. 6:1–23). Freed from sin's guilt and dominion, we are progressively delivered from the presence and power of sin. At our deaths, our souls at last will be perfected in holiness. At the return of Christ, our souls, reunited with glorified bodies, will be perfected in happiness.

The standard of all Christian living is the law of God. The Westminster Larger and Shorter catechisms give a searching, detailed, and practical exposition of the Ten Commandments. Freed by Christ from every kind of spiritual tyranny, we exercise our Christian f

...ing (1 Cor. 10.31). When we live to glorify God and not ourselves, we are answering the purpose for which God made us and redeemed us. It is in this kind of life alone that true and lasting joy, satisfaction, contentment, and pleasure are found.

## HOW DO REFORMED CHURCHES WORSHIP?

Worship is a special part of our life together as the church, a part about which God cares deeply. In the Bible, He gives us detailed instructions about public worship. God not only tells us what He wants us to do, He forbids us from worshiping Him in any "way not prescribed in the holy Scripture" (WCF, 21.1). The criteria that are so often applied to the public worship of God—cultural relevancy, evangelistic appeal, or emotional satisfaction—all proceed from a mistaken premise. Biblical public worship does not find its justification in what is thought to please me or the people around me, but in what is known to please God, according to what God has authorized in the Bible.

The beauty of biblical public worship is that when we worship God in God's way, we worship with the expectation that He draws near to bless His people. Our desire for personal satisfaction never determines what is or is not acceptable public worship. But God often blesses acceptable public worship to the satisfaction of His people's hearts.

Reformed churches long for three things in the public worship of God. First, they long for the Word of God to be central. We see this in the right emphasis that Reformed churches have given to the reading and preaching of the Word of God in public worship. Why? Because it is there that we look to God to convert lost sinners, and to confirm, comfort, and build up those who are already converted (see WLC, Q&A 191). Biblical public worship is a God-appointed means to build His kingdom outward and upward. Do you want to see sinners converted and saints maturing? Then aim for public worship that is biblical, and pray that God would bless that worship.

Second, Reformed churches long for the hearts of God's people to be engaged. Authentic public worship is a work of the heart. "Acceptable worship" is offered "with reverence and awe" because of who our great God is (Heb. 12:28–29). God calls us to worship Him with gladness, thanksgiving, and praise because "the LORD is good; his steadfast love endures forever, and his faithfulness to all generations" (Ps. 100:2, 4, 5). As these passages show, it is a profound sense of the holiness, goodness, and faithfulness of God that engages the heart. This is why biblical public worship is neither casual nor morose, but both reverent and joyful.

Third, Reformed churches long for the Spirit of God to be present in power in the public worship of God. Unless the Spirit works savingly in the hearts of the worshipers, no one will be converted and no one will grow in grace; the worshipers' hearts will remain cold and distant from God. Reformed churches do not look for the Spirit's activity in raucous, disorderly worship. Our standard is that "all things should be done decently and in order" (1 Cor. 14:40). Neither do Reformed churches look for the Spirit's activity in miracles, tongues, and prophecy. These gifts have ceased (see WCF 1.1). Reformed

Reformed churches.

Ultimately, the sole measure and standard of Reformed churches is Scripture. I urge you to read this book and the confessions of the Reformed churches in the spirit of those Berean men and women, who, when hearing the preaching of the apostle Paul, devoted themselves to "examining the Scriptures daily to see if these things were so" (Acts 17:11). May God direct you to a fuller understanding of His Word, and may that understanding prompt you to adore, serve, and praise the Savior and Head of the church.

—Dr. Guy Prentiss Waters
Associate Professor of New Testament
Reformed Theological Seminary, Jackson, Mississippi
March 2009

*Notes*

1   John Duncan, cited in William Knight, *Colloquia Peripatetica*, 5th ed (Edinburgh: David Douglas, 1879), 8.

2   William Ames, *The Marrow of Theology*, trans. John Dykstra Eusden (1968; repr., Grand Rapids: Baker, 1997), 77.

for offering such a kind foreword. He exemplifies what it means to be a Christian gentleman, and I thank the Lord that we have become friends.

I would like to thank several of my parishioners at the Oceanside United Reformed Church who helped to make this book a reality. Both Inwoo Lee and Wayde Gilliam encouraged me to write a brief introduction to what Reformed churches are all about as a means of educating the members of our congregation to be bolder in their witness, as well as a means of outreach in the community in which we minister, where we are the only Reformed congregation. Their passion for the gospel and for sharing it with others has been a great example for me. They also provided invaluable comments along the way and suggested many of the questions at the end of this book. I also need to thank another of my parishioners, Sarah Miranda, whose editorial help made this an even more readable manuscript. As well, the council of pastors, elders, and deacons at the Oceanside Church ceaselessly encourage me "diligently to teach and faithfully to defend" the doctrines of the Reformed confessions in writing as an extension of my ministry of the Word, even as I promised to do when I was ordained to the ministry of the Word and sacraments.

Four of my colleagues in the gospel ministry read the manuscript and offered constructive feedback as to the content and structure of the book. Revs. Kevin Efflandt and Jerrold Lewis were a blessing in this process, as was my former parishioner and now colleague Rev. Shane Lems, whose work ethic and sharp mind challenge me to write clearly and, I pray, compellingly. I am also grateful for Dr. Kim Riddlebarger's encouragement. He is a father in the faith to droves of us in Southern California who did not grow up in Reformed churches, just as he did not.

As always, I thank God for my devoted wife, Karajean, and my sons, Cyprian, Caiden, and Daxton, who remind me every day of the blessings of belonging to a Reformed church.

"Dad, who are these guys?" I remember my question and my dad's answer as if it were yesterday. I was a senior in high school and a new Christian, and I was sitting at the dining room table on a Sunday evening doing my homework while listening to the radio. As all good young Christians in my area were told to do by their youth pastors, I had the radio tuned to the large Christian radio station in Los Angeles County: KKLA. On came a show that began, curiously, with the sound of hoof beats. Then came the introduction: "Welcome to the White Horse Inn."[1] I had no idea what the four hosts were talking about that night, but apparently my dad did—"Oh, those are a bunch of Lutherans," he said.

I found out a couple of years later, while in college, that one of those on the show was, in fact, a Lutheran, but the others included a Baptist and two men who were something called "Reformed." This just added to the confusion. After all, in the circle of churches in which I was converted, worshiped, and eventually became a youth pastor, you either were a Christian—which meant you went to a

"Bible-believing, Spirit-filled" church like a Foursquare Church, Calvary Chapel, or a nondenominational church—or you were a "Catholic," meaning, Roman Catholic. I was aware of some other kinds of churches because at different times I liked a Presbyterian girl and even dated a Lutheran girl, but their churches were considered more or less Catholic because they were "dead," "traditional," or "ritualistic." I didn't have a category for "Reformed." However, a few years later and to the chagrin of some in my circle of family and friends—not the least of whom was the woman who is now my wife—I became one of "them."

Maybe you too are confused about all of the so-called "churches" dotting the religious landscape. As you drive down the road you see "Hometown Presbyterian Church," "Neighborhood Community Church," "Family Fellowship," and a host of others. Maybe you have seen or have heard secondhand of "Reformed" churches, but have never actually worshiped in one or investigated their beliefs. Perhaps you have heard some strange rumors about them. As you hold this book, you may be a little curious or you may even be a little critical. I can't complain; at least you're holding my book.

What are these churches that are called "Reformed" anyway? Why are they called "Reformed"? What do they believe? Where did they come from? What do they do that is different from what you are used to? These are great questions, and just the types of basic questions I hope to answer, or at least begin to answer, in this brief book.[2] As a former outsider to these churches and now a planter of a Reformed church in an area with no other church like it, I know where you are coming from.

The New Testament describes those who believe in Jesus Christ as pilgrims in this life (1 Peter 1:1; 2:11).[3] In your pilgrimage, you may be moving toward involvement in a Reformed church. If so, I want this book to make your pilgrimage as informed and smooth as possible.

To get a sense of the role I foresee for this book in a believer's

pew and the worship service begins. Likewise, a heavy-duty book of systematic theology or any title of the sixteenth- and seventeenth-century Reformed and Puritan theologians takes you to an even greater depth of experience.

While there are variations from one Reformed church to another, what I hope to communicate to you in this basic welcome to the Reformed churches as a whole can be summarized in three points. First, *Reformed churches are* Christian *churches*. They are Christian churches because they believe the Bible is the Word of God, that there is only one God who exists eternally as a Trinity, and that Jesus Christ our Savior is both God and man. Reformed churches hold these beliefs in common with all Christians in all times and places. In the words of Vincent of Lerins (d. 450), "We hold that faith which has been believed everywhere, always, by all."[4] Second, *Reformed churches are* Protestant *churches* along with Lutheran churches because they reject the claims of the pope to be the head of the church, acknowledging instead that Jesus Christ is the Head of *His* church, and that He rules and governs His church by His

Word and His Spirit, not by the dictates of men. Third, *Reformed churches are just that*—Reformed *churches.* They are a subset of Protestant churches in that they believe sinful humans are saved by grace alone, from eternity past to eternity future, and that we experience this grace of God earned for us by Christ alone when the Holy Spirit uses certain means that God has appointed in the church: the preaching of the Word of God, which is the Bible, and the celebration of the sacraments of baptism and the Lord's Supper.

My prayer in writing this book is that I can begin to clear up any misunderstandings you might have about what Reformed churches believe and even begin to open your eyes to a new world, a new way of looking at "the faith that was once for all delivered to the saints" (Jude 3). Frankly, I do not want you sitting at a table in confusion as I did so many years ago. I invite you to read this book as if we were in a conversation together as pilgrims on a road, discussing the Scriptures, church history, and the Christian life as understood by those branches of Christ's church that call themselves "Reformed."

Welcome to a Reformed church.

*Notes*

1  For more information about this program, visit http://www.whitehorseinn.org.

2  For further resources, see Appendix 2: "A Basic Bibliography."

3  On this theme of the people of God as pilgrims in this age, see Scott Nash, *The Church as a Pilgrim People: Hebrews–Revelation* (Macon, Ga.: Smyth & Helwys, 2001); O. Palmer Robertson, *God's People in the Wilderness: The Church in Hebrews* (Ross-shire, Scotland: Mentor, 2009); Joseph M. Shaw, *The Pilgrim People of God: Recovering a Biblical Motif* (Minneapolis: Augsburg Fortress, 1990).

4  Vincent of Lerins, *A Commonitory* 2.6, in *Nicene and Post-Nicene Fathers: Second Series, Vol. 11: Sulpitius Severus, Vincent of Lerins, John Cassian,* ed. Philip Schaff (1894; repr., Peabody, Mass.: Hendrickson Publishers, 2004), 132.

*Those who cannot remember the past are condemned to repeat it.*[1]

—George Santayana (1863–1952)

*To be ignorant of what occurred before you were born is to remain always a child.*[2]

—Cicero (106–43 BC)

I want to begin with a little history lesson. I know, I know, we enlightened moderns are not much into history; for most of us, it's a dry subject we hated in school. We care about the here and now, and are busy planning our futures. We think our time is the most important time in human history. Because of this, we are guilty of what Oxford University Professor C. S. Lewis (1898–1963) described as "chronological snobbery."[3]

This "snobbery" presents us with very real dangers. Since we live in a time when history is easily forgotten at best or dismissed as irrelevant at worst, we need to heed the words of the Spanish-American philosopher George Santayana and the Roman philosopher Cicero, as quoted above. It is important for us to take these words to heart, for if we do not know our past, we will suffer its tragic mistakes again and again, remaining like little children forever.

Scripture speaks in this way, as well. After Jeremiah prophesied the coming destruction of Jerusalem because of the rebelliousness of the people of God, he spoke of a way of escape: "Thus says the LORD: 'Stand by the roads, and look, and ask for the ancient paths, where the good way is; and walk in it, and find rest for your souls'" (Jer. 6:16). The faithful were to look backward to the "ancient paths," to the history of what God had done and said to His people in the past. Likewise, the Psalms abound in calls for God to work in the present because of what He did in the past. For instance, "O God, we have heard with our ears, our fathers have told us, what deeds you performed in their days, in the days of old" (Ps. 44:1; cf. Pss. 78, 105, 106, 107). History, then, is to guide the church in the present.

My purpose in this chapter is to help you appreciate that Reformed churches did not come out of nowhere. As I noted in the introduction, Reformed churches are Christian, Protestant, and Reformed. They are *Christian* because they trace their roots to the early church of the centuries after the apostles died (100–500). The Reformed churches—also known as "Calvinist" churches, after the theologian and pastor of Geneva, Switzerland, John Calvin (1509–1564)—are *Protestant* churches because, like the "Lutheran" churches—after the theologian and pastor in Wittenberg, Germany, Martin Luther (1483–1546)—they trace their roots to the sixteenth-century "Protestant Reformation" of the Roman Catholic Church in Europe.[4] They are *Reformed* churches because they emphasize certain doctrines that have a strong historical basis but are often neglected today.

## CHRISTIAN CHURCHES

Reformed churches are Christian churches because they trace their

to these, neither let him take ought from these."⁰

A part of joining with the Christian church and standing on the Word of God is confessing what are known as the ecumenical creeds of the ancient church—the Apostles', Nicene, and Athanasian creeds, as well as the Definition of Chalcedon. The Belgic Confession (1561) speaks of these, saying, "we do willingly receive the three creeds, namely, that of the Apostles, of Nice, and of Athanasius; likewise that which, conformable thereunto, is agreed upon by the ancient fathers" (Art. 9). Those things that are "conformable thereunto" are expressed in the Definition of Chalcedon (451). The Second Helvetic Confession, written by the Zurich pastor Heinrich Bullinger (1504–75) in 1561 and published in 1566, also lists the ancient creeds the Reformed churches receive: ". . . we freely profess, whatsoever things are defined out of the Holy Scriptures, and comprehended in the creeds, and in the decrees of those four first and most excellent councils—held at Nicaea, Constantinople, Ephesus and Chalcedon—together with blessed Athanasius's creed and all other creeds like to these, touching the mystery of the incarnation of our Lord Jesus Christ" (Art. 11).

These creeds are called "ecumenical." The term *ecumenical* comes from the Greek word *oikoumene*, which was used in the ancient world to describe the vastness of the Roman Empire. It is a way of describing the known world.[7] These creeds are ecumenical, or universal, because they have been received and believed by Christian churches in all times and in all places. Because you may be unfamiliar with them, it will be helpful to review briefly their history and content.

### The Apostles' Creed

I believe in God the Father, Almighty, Maker of heaven and earth.

And in Jesus Christ, His only begotten Son, our Lord; who was conceived by the Holy Spirit, born of the virgin Mary; suffered under Pontius Pilate; was crucified, dead, and buried; He descended into hell; the third day He rose again from the dead; He ascended into heaven, and sitteth at the right hand of God the Father Almighty; from thence He shall come to judge the living and the dead.

I believe in the Holy Spirit; I believe a holy catholic Church, the communion of saints; the forgiveness of sins; the resurrection of the body; and the life everlasting. Amen.[8]

Although it bears the title of their office, the apostles themselves did not write the Apostles' Creed. It developed over several centuries (100–700) as the ancient churches developed a practice that, at baptism, the adult candidate for baptism would confess his or her faith publicly. Scholars have showed that passages such as

Ephesians 4:4–6 were used as creeds at the baptism of new converts.[9] The first official version of the Apostles' Creed was used in Rome as early as the second century.[10] We can legitimately call this creed the Apostles' Creed because its ideas and phrases are

. . . first is of *God the Father* and our *creation*; the second, of *God the Son* and our *redemption*; the third, of *God the Holy Ghost* and our *sanctification*" (Q&A 24).[11]

### The Nicene Creed

I believe in one God, the Father Almighty, Maker of heaven and earth, and of all things visible and invisible.

And in one Lord Jesus Christ, the only-begotten Son of God, begotten of the Father before all worlds; God of God, Light of Light, very God of very God; begotten, not made, being of one substance with the Father, by whom all things were made. Who, for us men and for our salvation, came down from heaven and was Incarnate by the Holy Spirit of the virgin Mary, and was made man; and was crucified also for us under Pontius Pilate; He suffered and was buried; and the third day He rose again, according to the Scriptures; and ascended into heaven, and sitteth on the right hand of the Father; and He shall come again, with glory, to judge the living and the dead; whose kingdom shall have no end.

And I believe in the Holy Spirit, the Lord and Giver of life; who proceedeth from the Father and the Son; who with the Father and the Son together is worshipped and glorified; who spake by the prophets.

And I believe one holy catholic and apostolic Church. I acknowledge one baptism for the remission of sins; and I look for the resurrection of the dead, and the life of the world to come. Amen.[12]

The Nicene Creed was written in AD 325 at the ancient church's first ecumenical council, the Council of Nicea, the modern-day city of Iznik, Turkey.[13] Representatives from throughout the churches of the ancient world gathered to respond to and reject the false teaching of a preacher named Arius (250– 336).[14] Arius taught that the Son of God was not eternal, but was the first creation of God the Father (a doctrine espoused in modern days by the Jehovah's Witnesses). This meant that Jesus Christ was less divine than God the Father.

Later, at the second ecumenical council, the Council of Constantinople in AD 381, the churches responded to the false teaching of a group called the Macedonians, who said that the Holy Spirit was not fully God. It was then that the beautiful phrases about the Holy Spirit in the Nicene Creed were added to complete this great creed. For this reason, this creed is also called the Nicene-Constantinopolitan Creed.

Because of its importance in the ancient church's first two councils, its depth of teaching, and its purpose in protecting the church from false teaching about Jesus Christ and the Holy Spirit, the Nicene Creed is the most important of the ancient Christian creeds. Like the Apostles' Creed, the Nicene Creed is organized around the

(2) Which faith except every one do keep whole and undefiled, without doubt he shall perish everlastingly.

(3) And the catholic faith is this: That we worship one God in Trinity, and Trinity in Unity;

(27) So that in all things, as aforesaid, the Unity in Trinity and the Trinity in Unity is to be worshipped.

(28) He therefore that will be saved must thus think of the Trinity.

(29) Furthermore it is necessary to everlasting salvation that he also believe rightly the incarnation of our Lord Jesus Christ.

(44) This is the catholic faith, which except a man believe faithfully, he cannot be saved.[16]

The Athanasian Creed is named after Athanasius, who was a deacon in the church in Alexandria, Egypt.[17] Athanasius was one of the staunchest opponents of the teachings of Arius at the Council of Nicea. His firm stand is seen in this story about him: When he was told, "Athanasius, the world is against you," Athanasius replied, "Then Athanasius is against the world."

Like the Apostles' Creed, the Athanasian Creed most likely was not written by its namesake but was taken from his writings against Arius. These parts of his writings were compiled as a beautifully poetic creed some time between AD 500 and 800.

The Athanasian Creed is divided into two parts. The first is a detailed confession of the doctrine of the Trinity, affirming that we believe and worship one God in Unity and Unity in Trinity. The second part is a detailed confession of the doctrine of the person of Christ, affirming that there is one Lord Jesus Christ, who is both perfect God and perfect man. Both of these parts of the creed open with a statement of the necessity to believe in the triune nature of God and the two natures of Christ in order to have salvation.[18]

## *The Definition of Chalcedon*

> We, then, following the holy Fathers, all with one consent, teach men to confess one and the same Son, our Lord Jesus Christ, the same perfect in Godhead and also perfect in manhood; truly God and truly man, of a reasonable [rational] soul and body; consubstantial [coessential] with the Father according to the Godhead, and consubstantial with us according to the Manhood; in all things like unto us, without sin; begotten before all ages of the Father according to the

Godhead, and in these latter days, for us and for our salvation, born of the Virgin Mary, the Mother of God according to the Manhood; one and the same Christ, Son, Lord, Only-

prophets from the beginning [have declared] concerning him, and the Lord Jesus Christ himself has taught us, and the Creed of the holy Fathers has handed down to us.

Although the Belgic Confession explicitly names only the Apostles', Nicene, and Athanasian Creeds in its confession of the doctrine of the Trinity, it also speaks of "that which, conformable thereunto, is agreed upon by the ancient fathers" (Art. 9). One of the ancient church fathers' documents that agreed with the creeds was the Definition of Chalcedon. The Definition of Chalcedon was written in AD 451 at the fourth ecumenical council, the Council of Chalcedon, a city in modern-day Turkey. At this council, the churches of the ancient world gathered to respond to several different false teachings about our Lord Jesus Christ.[19]

One of those false teachings was Nestorianism. The followers of Nestorius taught that Christ's divine and human natures were so divided that Jesus Christ was two completely separate persons, not united in the one person of Christ. Another equally false teaching was that of Eutychianism. This belief system held that Christ's natures were so united in His person that the divine nature swallowed up the human nature, thus leaving one mixed nature. The third false teaching was that of Apollinarianism. This school taught that Jesus had a true human body and a "lower soul" (which animals have), but that the "higher soul" (which only humans have) was replaced by the eternal *logos* (the "Word" of John 1:1). This meant that Jesus Christ was not as fully human as we are. As Gregory of Nazianzus (325–389) so famously said in opposing this belief, "That which He has not assumed He has not healed."[20]

Again, theologians, pastors, and church leaders had to meet as an ecumenical council to respond to these teachings and confess what the Word of God taught on the essential doctrine of who Jesus Christ is. The Definition is one paragraph in which the church confessed to believe in one Lord Jesus Christ, who has two natures, divine and human.[21] This expression of the true humanity of Christ was stressed by calling Mary the "Mother [or "bearer"] of God according to the Manhood." She gave birth to the Son of God's human nature.

These four great creeds defined ancient Christianity against various errors for the first one thousand years of the church's existence until the rise of many more errors in the centuries just before the Protestant Reformation. Because Reformed churches believe these creeds, they are historical Christian churches.

## PROTESTANT CHURCHES

. . . our reformers have done no small service to the Church, in stirring up the world as from the deep darkness of ignorance, to read the Scriptures, in labouring diligently to make them better understood, and in happily throwing light on certain points of doctrine of the highest practical importance.[22]

Reformed churches are also Protestant, and they [23] G

the Roman Catholic Church's false teachings. The main teachings to which these reform-minded groups objected were Rome's insistence that the Bible was only one authority among many, including tradition and the pope, and the teaching that sinners were saved from their sin and God's wrath by cooperating with God's grace in doing good works. The protestations of the Reformers were that Scripture *alone* (*sola Scriptura*) was the ultimate authority in the church and that sinners are saved by God's grace *alone* (*sola gratia*), which is received through faith *alone* (*sola fide*), which is placed in Christ *alone* (*solus Christus*). These teachings, along with others, were expressed by both the Lutherans and the Reformed in various confessions of faith, such as the Augsburg Confession (1530) and the French Confession (1559), by which they bore witness to the world; and in various catechisms, such as Luther's Small Catechism (1529) and Calvin's Genevan Catechism (1545), by which they sought to instruct their churches.

These protestations against the Roman Catholic Church are important for us because many of the churches in our neighborhoods have become like the church the original Protestants reacted against so many years ago. Those first Protestants were known as evangelicals because they believed and preached the gospel of free grace. Today, many Protestant churches describe themselves as evangelical, but they have drifted far from the positions of the original Protestants. They still reject the pope, but the fact that many of them are governed by a pope-like, charismatic, and visionary leader calls out for protest and reformation. Likewise, evangelical churches claim to "just believe the Bible," but many of them merely follow their pastors' teachings and are filled with unbiblical traditions, such as altar calls and the "afterglow," a worship service after a worship service for serious believers who wish to exercise their "spiritual gifts." If we persist in "chronological snobbery," we are doomed to repeat the mistakes of the past and to remain childish in our outlook. The spirit of the original Protestants is still needed today.

## REFORMED CHURCHES

As time passed during the Reformation, the Lutherans and the Reformed became distinct camps within Protestantism with distinct confessions. The Protestants who followed Luther's teachings were derided as "Lutherans," while the Protestants who differed from Luther in several ways were derided as "Calvinists," though they called themselves "Reformed" Christians. This term, *Reformed*, was a shorthand way of saying, "Churches that are reformed according to the Word of God."

The Lutheran churches gathered various catechisms and confessions into one book, called the *Book of Concord* (1580), but the Reformed churches of various regions in Europe utilized different confessional standards.[25] Reformed churches could be found throughout Europe: in German-speaking Zurich, Switzerland, under Ulrich Zwingli (1484–1531) and later Heinrich Bullinger (1504–1575); in Strasbourg, under Martin Bucer (1491–1551); in Basel, under

archbishop of Canterbury, Thomas Cranmer (1489–1556). They also spread north to Poland, under Johannes à Lasco (1499–1560), and Heidelberg, Germany, under Elector Frederick III (1515–76), his main theologian, Zacharius Ursinus (1534–83), and his preacher, Caspar Olevianus (1536–87); and south, among the Waldensians in the mountains of northern Italy.

Eventually, two great collections of confessions became the basic statements of the Reformed churches. The Reformed churches from the continent of Europe held to the Three Forms of Unity: the Belgic Confession (1561), the Heidelberg Catechism (1563), and the Canons of Dort (1618–19). Those from Great Britain, known as Presbyterians, held to the Westminster Standards: the Westminster Confession of Faith (1647), the Westminster Larger Catechism (1648), and the Westminster Shorter Catechism (1648), to which were added the Directory for Publick Worship (1645) and the Form of Presbyterial Church Government (1645).

We speak of the Three Forms of Unity because there are three forms (*formulae*) expressing our beliefs (the Belgic Confession, the Heidelberg Catechism, and the Canons of Dort) and because these confessions, like all creeds, are meant to unify us in heart, soul, mind, and strength in what we believe the Word of God teaches.

### *The Belgic Confession*

> We all believe with the heart, and confess with the mouth, that there is one only simple and spiritual Being, which we call God; and that he is eternal, incomprehensible, invisible, immutable, infinite, almighty, perfectly wise, just, good, and the overflowing fountain of all good. (Art. 1)

The Belgic Confession of Faith was first published in 1561, having been written, among others, by Guido de Brès (1522–67), a French-speaking Reformed pastor in the southern Netherlands who later would die for his faith.[26] It was written on behalf of the persecuted Reformed churches throughout the Netherlands (now Holland, Belgium, and northern France) as an explanation of their Reformed Christian faith to the Roman Catholic king of Spain, Philip II, who ruled over the Netherlands at that time. Its immediate purpose was to demonstrate that the Reformed Christians were not trying to overthrow Philip and his government, as were some radical groups among the Anabaptists. Among the teachings of some Anabaptists was the belief that all earthly rulers were illegitimate and that only Jesus Christ was King.[27] To demonstrate that the Reformed in the Netherlands did not believe this, the confession sought to express that Reformation theology was simply the faith of the ancient church.

The content of this confession is as inspiring as the attitude of those Reformed Christians who confessed it. In an attached letter to the king, the Reformed Christians said: "But having the fear of God before our eyes, and being in dread of the warning of Jesus Christ,

fession is divided into six major parts according to the classic topics (*loci*) of theology: confessions about God (Arts. 1–13); confessions about man (Arts. 14–15); confessions about Christ (Arts. 16–21); confessions about salvation (Arts. 22–26); confessions about the church (Arts. 27–36); and confessions about the end (Art. 37).[29]

### *The Heidelberg Catechism*

**What is thy only comfort in life and in death?**
That I, with body and soul, both in life and in death, am not my own, but belong to my faithful Savior Jesus Christ, who with his precious blood has fully satisfied for all my sins, and redeemed me from all the power of the devil; and so preserves me that without the will of my Father in heaven not a hair can fall from my head; yea, that all things must work together for my salvation. Wherefore, by his Holy Spirit, he also assures me of eternal life, and makes me heartily willing and ready henceforth to live unto him. (Q&A 1)

The Heidelberg Catechism was written and published in 1563 in Heidelberg, Germany, at the request of Frederick III, ruler of the region in Germany called the Palatinate, in order to instruct his people in the Reformation's teachings. Although the word *catechism* might sound "catholic" to us, a catechism is simply a document that instructs in the basics of the Christian faith by using questions and answers; this is sometimes called the "Socratic method" of instruction.[30] The primary author of the Heidelberg Catechism was Zacharius Ursinus, a twenty-eight-year-old professor of theology. Others, such as Caspar Olevianus, a twenty-six-year-old preacher at the Holy Ghost Church in Heidelberg, assisted as a committee.[31]

Written in German, the catechism was intended solely for the region of the Palatinate, but it quickly underwent several editions and translations. It was translated into Latin (1563), Dutch (1563), English (1572), Hungarian (1577), French (1590), Greek (1609), Romansch (1613), Czech (1619), and Romanian (1648).[32] It became, and remains, the most popular, widely used, and comforting catechism of the Reformation period. It was even the first explanation of Reformed theology used in America when immigrants came here in the early 1600s.

The catechism explains the Christian faith in three parts, following the outline of the New Testament letter of the apostle Paul to the Romans. After questions 1–2 address the theme of the Christian's comfort and confidence in Jesus Christ and present an outline of the catechism, the rest of the catechism is structured in this way: guilt/sin (Q&A 3–11; Rom. 1:18–3:20); grace/salvation (Q&A 12–85; Rom. 3:21–11:36); and gratitude/service (Q&A 86–129; Rom. 12–16).[33]

## *The Canons of Dort*

> What, therefore, neither the light of nature nor the law could
> ~~do, that God, of and, through the operation of his Holy Spirit~~

written in 1618–19 in Dordrecht, Holland. After the Reformed
Christian faith became more established in the Netherlands, a great
controversy arose within the church there. A teacher of theology at
the University of Leiden, James Arminius (1560–1609), was accused
of teaching new doctrines contrary to the Belgic Confession and
Heidelberg Catechism.[34] After his death, more than forty of his followers wrote what was called *The Remonstrance* (1610), an official
protest to the government, outlining their theology and asking for
toleration. To give you the background for the Canons of Dort, it is
necessary to quote this document:

> **Article 1**: That God by an eternal and immutable decree
> has in Jesus Christ his Son determined before the founda-
> tion of the world *to save out of the fallen sinful human race*
> *those in Christ, for Christ's sake, and through Christ who*
> *by the grace of the Holy Spirit shall believe in this his Son*
> Jesus Christ and persevere in this faith and obedience of
> faith; and on the other hand to leave the incorrigible and
> unbelieving in sin and under wrath and condemn (them)

as alienate from Christ—according to the word of the holy gospel in John 3:36: "He that believeth on the Son hath eternal life, and whosoever is disobedient to the Son shall not see life, but the wrath of God abideth on him," and also other passages of the Scriptures.

**Article 2**: That in agreement with this *Jesus Christ the Savior of the world died for all men and for every man, so that he merited reconciliation and forgiveness of sins for all* through the death of the cross; yet so that no one actually enjoys this forgiveness of sins except the believer—also according to the word of the gospel of John 3:16: "God so loved the world that he gave his only-begotten Son that whosoever believeth in him shall not perish but have eternal life." And in the first epistle of John 2:2: "He is the propitiation for our sins; and not only for ours, but also for the sins of the whole world."

**Article 3**: That man does not have saving faith of himself nor by the power of his own free will, since he in the state of apostasy and sin can not of and through himself think, will or do any good which is truly good (such as is especially saving faith); but that it is necessary that he be regenerated by God, in Christ, through his Holy Spirit, and renewed in understanding, affections or will, and all powers, in order that he may rightly understand, meditate upon, will, and perform that which is truly good, according to the word of Christ, John 15:5: "Without me ye can do nothing."

**Article 4**: That this grace of God is the commencement, progression, and completion of all good, also in so far that regenerate man cannot, apart from this prevenient or assisting, awakening, consequent and coop...

**Article 5**: That those who are incorporated into Jesus Christ and thereby become partakers of his life-giving Spirit have abundant strength to strive against satan, sin, the world, and their own flesh and to obtain the victory; it being well understood (that this is) through the assistance of the grace of the Holy Spirit, and that Jesus Christ assists them through his Spirit in all temptations, extends the hand, and—if only they are prepared for warfare and desire his help and are not negligent—keeps them standing, so that by no cunning or power of satan can they be led astray or plucked out of Christ's hands, according to the word of Christ, John 10, "No one shall pluck them out of my hands." *But whether they can through negligence fall away from the first principle of their life in Christ, again embrace the present world, depart from the pure doctrine once given to them, lose the good conscience, and neglect grace, must first be more carefully determined from the Holy Scriptures before we shall be able to teach this with the full persuasion of our heart.*[35]

Because of this teaching, a synod, that is, a gathering of churches, was called with pastors and theologians from throughout the Netherlands and from throughout Europe: Great Britain, the Palatinate, Hesse, Zurich, Berne, Basel, Schaffhausen, Geneva, Bremen, Emden, and Nassau-Wetteravia; delegates from France and Brandenburg were invited but were prevented from attending.[36] Of this synod, the English Puritan John Owen (1616–1683) said, "The divines of that assembly . . . were esteemed of the best that all the reformed churches of Europe (that of France excepted) could afford."[37]

The result of this synod was the rejection of Arminianism in the Canons of Dort. A "canon" is simply a "rule," so the Canons of Dort are the rules of faith written by the Synod of Dort. These canons are the official teachings of the Reformed churches on what are commonly called the Five Points of Calvinism, which are often summarized by the acronym TULIP.[38] It is important to note, though, that the canons were composed as a response to false teaching, not to summarize the entire Reformed faith. The Belgic Confession and Heidelberg Catechism were assumed to accomplish that task.

Since the canons responded to the points of the Arminians, their teachings are divided into four parts: unconditional election; limited atonement; man's total depravity and God's irresistible grace; and the preservation/perseverance of the saints.

### The Westminster Standards

**What is the chief end of man?**
Man's chief end is to glorify God, and to enjoy him forever.
(WSC, Q&A 1)

The Westminster Standards—the Westminster Confession of Faith (1647), the Westminster Larger Catechism (1648), and the Westminster Shorter Catechism (1648)—were written during the brief period of Puritan ascendancy in mid sevent...

...to unite the kingdoms of England, Scotland, and Ireland, the delegates to the assembly came to see that something more was needed. In the summer of 1644, a committee was created to write a confession of the united Reformed faith in Great Britain.[39]

The Westminster Confession of Faith follows a classic order of Christian doctrine, as exemplified in the aforementioned Belgic Confession: Holy Scripture (Chap. 1); God (Chaps. 2–5); man (Chaps. 6–7); Christ (Chap. 8); salvation (Chaps. 9–24); the church (Chaps. 25–31); and the intermediate state and the end (Chaps. 32–33).

Likewise, both the Larger and Shorter catechisms open with an introductory set of questions and then move to the heart of their teaching: introduction (WLC, Q&A 1–5; WSC, Q&A 1–3); doctrine (WLC, Q&A 6–90; WSC, Q&A 4–38); and duty (WLC, Q&A 91–196; WSC, Q&A 39–107).

## CONCLUSION

The foregoing demonstrates that the churches of the Protestant Reformation known as Reformed churches have deep roots historically and theologically. These roots are the ancient Christian creeds and the Reformed confessions and catechisms. Because these creeds, confessions, and catechisms are based on the teachings of the Bible, Reformed churches have deep biblical roots, as well. These roots give stability to modern Christians who have become detached from history, and maturity to those who were once like children.

## Notes

1  George Santayana, *The Life of Reason*, Great Books in Philosophy (1905–1906; repr., Amherst, N.Y.: Prometheus Books, 1998), 82.

2  Cicero, *De Oratore*, sec. 120. The Latin text is as follows *Nescire autem quid ante quam natus sis acciderit, id est semper esse puerum.*

3  C. S. Lewis, *Surprised by Joy: The Shape of My Early Life* (1955; repr., New York: Harcourt Trade Publishers, 1966), 204, 205, 211, 214.

4  On the history of these titles, see Diarmaid MacCulloch, *The Reformation: A History* (New York: Penguin, 2003), xix–xx.

5  For a basic history of the early centuries of the Christian church, see Henry Chadwick, *The Early Church* (1967; repr., New York: Penguin, 1990).

6  Athanasius, "Festal Letter 39.6," in *Nicene and Post-Nicene Fathers: Second Series, Vol. 4: Athanasius: Select Words and Letters*, ed. Archibald Robertson (1892; repr., Peabody, Mass.: Hendrickson Publishers, 2004), 552.

7  Walter Bauer, *A Greek-English Lexicon of the New Testament and Other Early Christian Literature*, trans. and rev. William F. Arndt, F. Wilbur Gingrich, and Frederick W. Danker (Chicago: University of Chicago Press, 1979), 561.

8  *Psalter Hymnal* (Grand Rapids: Christian Reformed Church, 1976), 3.

9  F. F. Bruce, *The Epistles to the Colossians, to Philemon, and to the Ephesians*, New International Commentary on the New Testament (Grand Rapids: Eerdmans, 1984), 335–336.

10 For an extensive history of the Apostles' Creed, see Liuwe H. Westra, *The Apostles' Creed: Origin, History, and Some Early Commentaries*, Instrumenta Patristica et Mediaevalia 43 (Turnhout, Belgium: Brepolis Publishers, 2002).

11 On this basic description of the creed, see Daniel R. Hyde, *The Good Confession: An Exploration of the Christian Faith* (Eugene, Ore.: Wipf & Stock, 2006), 19.

12 *Psalter Hymnal*, 4.

13 For studies of the Nicene Creed, see T. F. Torrance, *The Trinitarian Faith: The Evangelical Theology of the Ancient Catholic Church* (Edinburgh: T&T Clark, 1988); L. Charles Jackson, *Faith of our Fathers: A Study of the Nicene Creed* (Moscow, Ida.: Canon Press, 2007).

Adam and Charles Black, 1964). For an introduction to Athanasius, see Thomas G. Weinandy, *Athanasius: A Theological Introduction*, Great Theologians Series (Hampshire, England: Ashgate, 2007).

18 On this basic description of the Athanasian Creed, see Hyde, *The Good Confession*, 20.

19 For a basic exposition of the doctrines taught in the Definition of Chalcedon, see Daniel R. Hyde, *God With Us: Knowing the Mystery of Who Jesus Is* (Grand Rapids: Reformation Heritage Books, 2007).

20 Gregory of Nazianzus, *Epistle 101: To Cledonius the Priest Against Apollinarius*, in *Nicene and Post-Nicene Fathers: Second Series, Vol. 7: Cyril of Jerusalem, Gregory Nazianzen*, trans. Charles Gordon Brown and James Edward Swallow (1894; repr., Peabody, Mass.: Hendrickson Publishers, 2004), 440.

21 On this basic description of the Definition of Chalcedon, see Hyde, *The Good Confession*, 20–21.

22 John Calvin, *The Necessity of Reforming the Church* (Audubon, N.J.: Old Paths Publications, 1994), 25.

23 For some basic introductions to the Protestant Reformation, see Euan Cameron, *The European Reformation* (Oxford, England: Clardendon Press, 1991); Lewis W. Spitz, *The Renaissance and Reformation Movements*, 2 vols. (1971; rev. ed., St. Louis: Concordia, 1987).

24 MacCulloch, *The Reformation*, xx.

25 On the *Book of Concord*, see *The Book of Concord: The Confessions of the Evangelical Lutheran Church*, ed. Robert Kolb and Timothy J. Wengert, trans.

Charles Arand, Eric Gritsch, Robert Kolb, William Russell, James Schaaf, Jane Strohl, and Timothy J. Wengert (Minneapolis: Fortress Press, 2000); *Sources and Contexts of the Book of Concord*, ed. Robert Kolb and James A. Nestingen (Minneapolis: Fortress Press, 2001).

26 On the authorship of the Belgic Confession, see Nicolaas H. Gootjes, *The Belgic Confession: Its History and Sources*, Texts & Studies in Reformation & Post-Reformation Thought, gen. ed. Richard A. Muller (Grand Rapids: Baker Academic, 2007); Daniel R. Hyde, *With Heart and Mouth: An Exposition of the Belgic Confession* (Grandville, Mich.: Reformed Fellowship, 2008).

27 For a basic introduction to the Anabaptists, see William R. Estep, *The Anabaptist Story: An Introduction to Sixteenth-Century Anabaptism* (Grand Rapids: Eerdmans, 1996).

28 "Dedicatory Epistle to Philip II," trans. Alastair Duke, cited in Hyde, *With Heart and Mouth*, 500–501.

29 On this basic description of the Belgic Confession, see Hyde, *The Good Confession*, 22. For a more comprehensive history and commentary, see Hyde, *With Heart and Mouth*.

30 The word *catechism* comes from the Greek verb *katēcheō*, which occurs eight times in the New Testament (Luke 1:4; Acts 18:25; 21:21, 24; Rom. 2:18; 1 Cor. 14:19; Gal. 6:6 [twice]).

31 *The Church's Book of Comfort*, ed. Willem Van't Spijker, trans. Gerrit Bilkes (Grand Rapids: Reformation Heritage Books, 2009), 27–61; Lyle D. Bierma with Charles D. Gunnoe Jr., Karin Y. Maag, and Paul W. Fields, *An Introduction to the Heidelberg Catechism: Sources, History, and Theology*, Texts & Studies in Reformation & Post-Reformation Thought (Grand Rapids: Baker Academic, 2005), 49–74.

32 Bierma, *An Introduction to the Heidelberg Catechism*, 103–117.

33 On this basic description of the Heidelberg Catechism, see Hyde, *The Good Confession*, 22–23.

34 On Arminius, see W. Robert Godfrey, "Who Was Arminius?" *Modern Reformation* 1:3 (May/June 1992): 5–7, 24; Richard A. Muller, *God, Creation, and Providence in the Thought of Jacob Arminius: Sources and Directions of Scholastic Protestantism in the Era of Early Orthodoxy* (Grand Rapids: Baker, 1991); and "Arminius and the Reformed Tradition," *Westminster Theological Journal* 70:1 (Spring 2008): 19–48.

35 *Crisis in the Reformed Churches: Essays in Commemoration of the Great Synod of Dort, 1618–19*, ed. Peter Y. De Jong (Grandville, Mich.: Reformed Fellowship, 2008), 207–209. Italicized portions are the areas of controversy. One should note

that Article 3 in and of itself is not objectionable, and this is why the Canons of Dort have a "Third and Fourth Head of Doctrine" combined.

36 For the names of these delegates, see *Crisis in the Reformed Churches,* 213–21.

37 John Owen, "The Nature of Apostasy from the Profession of the Gospel and the Punishment of Apostates

*The banishments, prisons, racks, exiles, tortures and countless other persecutions plainly demonstrate that our desire and conviction is not carnal, for we would lead a far easier life if we did not embrace and maintain this doctrine. But having the fear of God before our eyes, and being in dread of the warning of Jesus Christ, who tells us that He shall forsake us before God and His Father if we deny Him before men, we suffer our backs to be beaten, our tongues to be cut, our mouths to be gagged and our whole body to be burnt, for we know that he who would follow Christ must take up his cross and deny himself. . . . And because we are persecuted as if we were not only enemies of your throne and the commonwealth, but also enemies of God and His Church, we humbly pray you to judge this by the Confession of faith, which we lay before you and which we are ready and willing, if necessary, to seal with our own blood. From this Confession we trust that you will see that we are wrongly called schismatics, promoters of disunity, rebels and*

*heretics, for we not only uphold and profess the chief heads of
the Christian faith, comprehended in the Symbolum or Creeds,
but also the whole teaching, revealed by Jesus Christ, for our
life, justification and salvation, proclaimed by the evangelists
and apostles, sealed with the blood of so many martyrs and
preserved pure and complete by the primitive Church.*[1]

—Guido de Brès, *Letter to King Philip II*

The story goes that a Dutch Reformed Christian once asked one
of his nondenominational Christian friends the following question: "So, what is your church's confession of faith?" The evangelical replied simply, "The Bible." The Dutchman was a bit puzzled, so he said, "But the Bible is so big."

This apocryphal story amusingly illustrates that while every Christian professes to believe the Bible, the real question is this: What does an individual Christian or a Christian church profess to believe the Bible *teaches*? After all, Christians of all sorts will readily swear allegiance to the Bible as the Word of God, but they may have vastly different understandings of such matters as how God created us, how God saves us, how the Holy Spirit brings gifts to the church, and how and when the Lord Jesus Christ will come again.[2]

As the opening chapter showed, Reformed churches teach and confess the ancient Christian creeds and Reformed confessions because their tenets come straight from the Bible and Christians have believed them over the centuries. To be a Reformed church, then, is to be a biblical church—but also a confessional church. This means that what Reformed churches believe to be the foundational truths of God's Holy Word are stated in public documents called creeds (Apostles', Nicene, and Athanasian, as well as the Definition of Chalcedon), catechisms (Heidelberg, Westminster Larger and Shorter), confessions (Belgic and Westminster), and canons (Canons of Dort).

How do we understand the relationship between the Word of God and these documents? On behalf of the sessions of Reformed

confessions are faithful expressions of what the Bible teaches.

Many Reformed churches, such as the one in which I minister, utilize what is called a "Form of Subscription," in which ministers sign their names to a document, promising their loyalty to the Word of God and their intention to teach it as expressed in the confessions. In my Form of Subscription, I said that I "sincerely and in good conscience before the Lord, declare by this [my] subscription that [I] heartily believe and [am] persuaded that all the articles and points of doctrine contained in the [Three Forms of Unity] do fully agree with the Word of God. [I] promise therefore diligently to teach and faithfully to defend the aforesaid doctrine, without either directly or indirectly contradicting the same by [my] public preaching or writing."[4] This illustrates how the Reformed churches use the creeds and confessions to guide their beliefs and practices.

## "NO CREED BUT CHRIST"

That Reformed churches are confessional is extremely important, because many churches and groups in our day, such as Calvary

Chapel, the Foursquare Church, and the Assemblies of God, say they are Christian and Protestant churches rooted in the Reformation. But while it may be true that a "family tree" could be traced from these churches back to the Reformation, they are not reformational churches because they are not confessional churches. They are related—and I say this with the utmost respect—only as a distant cousin would be considered a part of one's family. In fact, these churches say something like, "We believe no creed but Christ," or they believe that having creeds and confessions is nothing but a Roman Catholic practice.

Yet even these "just the Bible" churches have "statements of faith." For example, the Calvary Chapel movement has produced a book titled *Calvary Chapel Distinctives*, in which its founder, Chuck Smith, lists among the beliefs of Calvary Chapel:

- The "Moses Model" of ministry
- An additional work of the Spirit in empowering the believer beyond the indwelling of the Spirit
- A relaxed, casual style of worship
- The pre-tribulational rapture of the church
- "Balance" on nonessential issues, such as Calvinism and Arminianism.[5]

Despite claims that the creeds and confessions are unbiblical, that they are merely Roman Catholic traditions, or that they stifle the Spirit of God in the life of God's people, they are, in fact, biblical and beneficial.[6] Let's look briefly at these two traits.

## BIBLICAL

First, creeds and confessions are *biblical*. This is illustrated by the fact that the Old Testament people of God confessed their faith every morning and evening with the words of Deuteronomy 6:4, the basic confession of the Old Testament: "Hear, O Israel: the LORD our God: the LORD is one." We also learn that the Israelites

God (Matt. 16:16). This was the basic creed of the New Testament. Paul went on to elaborate on this in places such as 1 Corinthians 15:3–4, where he summarized the faith of the church in this creed: "Christ died for our sins in accordance with the Scriptures . . . he was buried . . . he was raised on the third day in accordance with the Scriptures." In the previously referenced Ephesians 4:4–6, Paul gave what many scholars believe to be a creed that was recited when a new convert was baptized: "There is one body and one Spirit . . . one hope . . . one Lord, one faith, one baptism, one God and Father." One last example of a New Testament creed is 1 Timothy 3:16, where Paul wrote to the young pastor Timothy, saying, "Great indeed, we confess, is the mystery of godliness: He was manifested in the flesh, vindicated by the Spirit, seen by angels, proclaimed among the nations, believed on in the world, taken up in glory."

While these texts from the Old and the New Testament are not as extensive as the creeds that were written by the ancient church fathers or the confessions of the Reformation, they show that there was a basic body of belief that the people of God confessed as the truth. Based on this fact, the church fathers and Reformers expressed the truth of the Word in their contexts in order to make clear what they believed.

Thus, creeds and confessions are not statements of stuffy "dead orthodox" churches or Roman Catholic churches. Instead, Christians throughout the millennia have written and recited creeds to express the faith that lived in their hearts. The Bible teaches us that, as the people of God, we have something to confess to the world. The slogan "No creed but Christ" actually hinders the church because, as one writer has said, "A creedless church cannot long exist."[7] Without something to confess, our faith is empty and meaningless to a world in need of Christ and the answers He gives to our lives.

## BENEFICIAL

Not only are creeds and confessions biblical, following the scriptural pattern of expressing core beliefs, they are *beneficial* in many ways. According to the New Testament, the church is to be unified. Paul speaks of glorifying God "with one voice," "standing firm in one spirit," and "with one mind striving side by side for the faith of the gospel" (Rom. 15:5–6; Phil. 1:27). The church also needs a clear standard of truth. Because the church has ever existed amid false doctrines and philosophies, under the threat of being "tossed to and fro by the waves and carried about by every wind of doctrine" (Eph. 4:14), it needs to be taught the essential truths of the Word of God; in that way, it can better "contend for the faith that was once for all delivered to the saints" (Jude 3). For this reason, Paul preached "the whole counsel of God" (Acts 20:27) and spoke of Gentile Romans who were slaves to sin coming to be "obedient from the heart to the standard of teaching to which you were committed" (Rom. 6:17).

Paul also wrote to Timothy that he should "follow the pattern of the sound words" (2 Tim. 1:13). The creeds and confessions of the church can help in carrying out all of these mandates by establishing a common confession of the faith

of the Word of God to those outside the church.

## CONCLUSION

The creeds and confessions are the official public faith of the Reformed churches. To fully answer the question, "What is a Reformed church?" you must read our historical creeds and confessions. A simple summary, such as this book, cannot do full justice to the breadth of the Reformed faith, but can only introduce you to major emphases.

I recognize, though, that a short introduction to our beliefs may persuade you to stop looking in our church windows and to walk in the front door. Therefore, in the chapters that follow, I exposit a few of the main points that make Reformed churches what they are: the authority of Scripture; the story of Scripture as an account of God's unfolding covenants; redemption coming by God's grace alone, through faith alone, in Christ alone; growth in grace through the process of sanctification; the distinguishing marks that make a church a true church; a desire to meet with God in worship according to His Word; and the means by which we come to experience God's grace: the preaching of the gospel and administration of the two sacraments. I have chosen these emphases because they are stressed by our confessions.

Yet, in seeing the various trees, there is always the risk of missing the entire forest. Because I will highlight only some of the points that are emphasized in our confessions, I wholeheartedly encourage you to read the Three Forms of Unity—the Belgic Confession, the Heidelberg Catechism, and the Canons of Dort—and the Westminster Standards—the Westminster Confession of Faith, the Westminster Larger Catechism, and the Westminster Shorter Catechism—to find out for yourself what a Reformed church is all about in its breadth and depth.

*Notes*

1  Cited in Daniel R. Hyde, *With Heart and Mouth: An Exposition of the Belgic Confession* (Grandville, Mich.: Reformed Fellowship, 2008), 500–501, 502.

2  Daniel R. Hyde, *The Good Confession: An Exploration of the Christian Faith* (Eugene, Ore.: Wipf & Stock, 2006), 7–28.

3  M. J. Bosma, *Exposition of Reformed Doctrine* (1907; fourth ed., Grand Rapids: Smitter, 1927), 1.

4  *Psalter Hymnal* (Grand Rapids: Christian Reformed Church, 1976), 117.

5  Chuck Smith, *Calvary Chapel Distinctives: The Foundational Principles of the Calvary Chapel Movement* (Costa Mesa, Calif.: The Word for Today, 2000). For the history of Calvary Chapel, see Chuck Smith and Tal Brooke, *Harvest: Gang Members, Drug Addicts, Mental Patients, Society's Rejects . . . Chuck Smith's Amazing Story of Calvary Chapel and the Unlikely Leaders God Called* (Costa Mesa, Calif.: The Word for Today, 2005).

6  For a fuller explanation of the issue of having creeds and confessions, see Hyde, *The Good Confession*, 7–28.

7  R. B. Kuiper, *As to Being Reformed* (second ed., Grand Rapids: Eerdmans, 1926), 111.

*How firm a foundation, ye saints of the Lord,*
*Is laid for your faith in His excellent Word!*
*What more can He say than to you He hath said,*
*You, who unto Jesus for refuge have fled?*[1]

—John Rippon

**W**hich came first, the chicken or the egg? The classic conundrum gets us thinking about the issue of origins. If we opine that the chicken came first, we're told, "But chickens hatch from eggs." If we declare that the egg came first, we're told, "But eggs are laid by chickens." You get the point—origins can be hard to determine.

This conundrum is reminiscent of the debate over the foundational issue of the Protestant Reformation—authority. At the time of the Reformation, the Roman Catholic Church had come to believe in two coequal sources of authority in the church: Scripture and tradition.[2] Since the pope had ultimate say on how these two authorities were interpreted, Rome eventually came to speak of the church as giving birth to the Scriptures. The Council of Trent, on April 8, 1546, issued the following decree regarding the gospel Jesus Christ commanded His apostles to preach:

> [It is] contained in the written books, and the unwritten traditions which, received by the Apostles from the mouth of Christ himself, or from the Apostles themselves, the Holy Ghost dictating, have come down even unto us, transmitted as it were from hand to hand: [the Synod] following the examples of the orthodox Fathers, receives and venerates with an equal affection of piety and reverence, all the books both of the Old and of the New Testament—seeing that one God is the author of both—as also the said traditions, as well those appertaining to faith as to morals, as having been dictated, either by Christ's own word of mouth, or by the Holy Ghost, and preserved in the Catholic Church by a continuous succession.[3]

The Protestant Reformers, on the other hand, spoke of the Word of God, which was written as "Scripture," as giving birth, form, and shape to the church. Martin Luther spoke colorfully when he said, "The Scripture is the womb from which are born the divine truth and the church."[4] The early Swiss Reformation document, the Ten Theses of Berne (1528), opened with these words: "The holy catholic church, whose sole head is Christ, has been begotten from the Word of God, in which also it continues, nor does it listen to the voice of any stranger."[5] After all, the Scriptures say the church is "built on the foundation of the apostles and prophets" (Eph 2:20), not the other way around.

In this chapter, I want to begin our journey through some of the fundamental themes of Reformed Christianity, beginning with the belief that the Scriptures are the final and highest authority in the Christian church in all areas of its faith and life.

...church because of the Word's own insistence that this is true. We see this authority in Scripture's repeated calls for man to honor the Word of God by neither adding to it nor taking away from it.

For example, after God redeemed His people out of Egypt (Ex. 12:33–42) and brought them through the Red Sea on dry ground (Ex. 14), He led them to Mount Sinai, where He made a sacred covenant with them, promising that He would be their God and they would be His people (Ex. 19–24). After the Israelites wandered in the wilderness for forty years, God renewed this covenant with them. This is what the book of Deuteronomy is about. The word *Deuteronomy* comes from two Greek words, *deuteros*, or "second," and *nomos*, or "law." It is the account of the second giving of the covenant law to the people of God. When God renewed His covenant, He said to His people through Moses, "You shall not add to the word that I command you, nor take from it, that you may keep the commandments of the LORD your God that I command you" (Deut. 4:2). Later, while prescribing the place of worship and warning His people not to worship another god, He said: "Everything that I command you, you shall be careful to do. You shall not add to it or take from it" (Deut. 12:32). There was even a proverb among the Israelites, which said: "Every word of God proves true; he is a shield to those who take refuge in him. Do not add to his words, lest he rebuke you and you be found a liar" (Prov. 30:5–6). Israel's faith and life were to be governed not by their desires or traditions, but by the Word of the Lord who saved them. As He told them during their wilderness journey, "man does not live by bread alone, but man lives by every word that comes from the mouth of the LORD" (Deut. 8:3).

Later, in the "fullness of time . . . God sent forth his Son" (Gal. 4:4), as Paul says. The writer to the Hebrews compares and contrasts God's speech in the Old Testament with that of the New Testament, saying, "Long ago, at many times and in many ways, God spoke to our fathers by the prophets, but in these last days he has spoken to us by his Son" (Heb. 1:1–2). God climactically revealed Himself to the world in the Word incarnate, our Lord Jesus Christ (John 1:1–18). The entire Old Testament was written as a prophetic witness of God's coming in the flesh (Luke 24:25–27, 44–47; John 5:39), and the entire New Testament was written as a testimony of what He did on earth. The Gospels explain His ministry while on earth, Acts explains His continued ministry by the Holy Spirit through the church, and the Epistles and Revelation interpret the meaning of His work for us as Christians in all ages. It is no coincidence, then, that the last book of the Bible, in its climactic verses, says, "I warn everyone who hears the words of the prophecy of this book: if anyone adds to them, God will add to him the plagues described in this book, and if anyone takes away from the words of the book of this prophecy, God will take away his share in the tree of life and in the holy city, which are described in this book" (Rev. 22:18–19).

The Reformed confessions bear witness to this truth that the Scriptures are our highest and ultimate authority. When the Westminster Larger Catechism asks, "What is the Word of God?" it answers, "The holy scripts     f th   Old   d N     T

Belgic Confession spends six of its thirty-seven articles on the issue of what is the Word of God, while the Westminster Confession of Faith opens with one of the most moving expressions of what the Word of God is, both of which I will quote substantially below.

## REVELATION

The Belgic Confession opens by confessing what the Bible says about God (Art. 1). Then, in Articles 2–7, it speaks of the Word of God. In Article 2, the Belgic Confession proclaims that the Word of God is the clearest revelation of Himself that God has given to His creatures. We believe that the God who created all things is not unknowable, but is knowable in and through His Holy Word. In this Word, He reveals Himself, that is, shows Himself to us in a clear and open way. God reveals Himself in a basic way in creation (Rom. 1:20), but the Belgic Confession says that by means of Scripture we can know the one true God "more clearly and fully . . . as far as is necessary for us to know in this life, to his glory and our salvation" (Art. 2). These words are rooted in Psalm 19. While "the heavens declare the glory of God, and the sky above proclaims his handiwork" (Ps. 19:1), the laws and precepts of God in His Word reveal Him in a more personal way: they revive the soul and make wise (v. 7); they rejoice the heart and enlighten the eyes (v. 8). Because of this, the psalmist says, "More to be desired are they than gold, even much fine gold; sweeter also than honey and drippings of the honeycomb" (v. 10).

While the Belgic Confession opens with God and then speaks of how He has revealed Himself in His Word, the Westminster Confession begins with the reality that God has revealed Himself in His Word before it goes on to speak about the God who is revealed in Scripture: "Although the light of nature, and the works of creation and providence, do so far manifest the goodness, wisdom, and power of God, as to leave men inexcusable; yet are they not sufficient to give that knowledge of God, and of his will, which is necessary unto salvation; therefore it pleased the Lord, at sundry times, and in divers manners, to reveal himself, and to declare that his will unto his Church" (1.1).

This article brings us great spiritual benefit. You see, it brings out just how personal our God is: He has "reveal[ed] *himself*." In His Word, as in His creation and providential care, we learn that our God is good, wise, and powerful, but most especially in His Word we learn about what is "necessary unto salvation." In this we come to know God *Himself*. J. I. Packer expressed the wonder of this truth when he asked: "Why has God spoken? He is self-sufficient, and does not need men's gifts or service (Acts 17:25); to what end, then, does He bother to speak to us? The truly staggering answer which the Bible gives to this question is that God's purpose in revelation is to *make friends* with us" (emphasis in original).[7]

It is this revelation of God, by God, that sets Christianity apart from all other religions. In all other religions, man speaks of god or the gods he has created and worships, but Christianity holds that

*men of God spake as they were moved by the Holy Ghost*" (BC, Art. 3). Here the Belgic Confession quotes from 2 Peter 1:20–21. These words speak of Scripture originating in the will of God, not the will of men. The apostle Paul spoke similarly when he said, "All Scripture is breathed out by God" (2 Tim. 3:16). The Greek word translated as "breathed out by God" (or "inspired by God," NASB) is *theopneustos*. This word emphasizes, as Peter's words do, that the origin of the Scriptures is in God's speech, not ours.

As I noted earlier, God's revelation is amazing because it is personal. Furthermore, this intimate Word that God spoke to His servants through the ages was written down because of His personal love for us. As the Belgic Confession says, "God, from a special care which he has for us and our salvation, commanded his servants, the Prophets and Apostles, to commit his revealed Word to writing" (Art. 3).

This truth that God's revelation was committed to writing by His own direction was expressed magnificently in the Westminster Confession of Faith, which elaborates on the terse sentence of the Belgic Confession: ". . . therefore it pleased the Lord, at sundry times, and in divers manners, to reveal himself, and to declare that his will unto his Church; and afterwards, for the better preserving and propagating of the truth, and for the more sure establishment and comfort of the Church against the corruption of the flesh, and the malice of Satan and of the world, to commit the same wholly unto writing" (1.1).

God had His breathed-out Word written down on pages so that His truth would be preserved among His people and propagated among the nations. Further, He gave His inspired Word to establish us in comfort against the assaults of our three deadly enemies: the world, the flesh, and the Devil.

## CANONICITY

God has revealed Himself and has committed His Word to writing, but a question remains: "*Where* is God's written Word found?" After all, there are many competing holy books among the religions of the world. Judaism has the *Tanach*, the Law, the Prophets, and the Writings of the Old Testament; Islam has the *Qur'an* (and the *Hadith* for Sunni Muslims); Hinduism has the *Bhagavad Gita*, the *Upanishads*, and the *Vedas*; Taoism has the *Tao-te-ching*; and Confucianism has *The Analects*. Even among Christians there is no consensus, as the Roman Catholic Church and Eastern Orthodoxy recognize the Old and New Testaments along with the books of the Apocrypha, while Protestants recognize only the Old and New Testaments.[8]

As part of the Protestant tradition, Reformed churches believe the inspired, revealed Word of God is found in the sixty-six books of the Old and New Testaments. These are what we call the "canonical" books, or, simply, "the canon." The word *canon* comes from the Greek word *kanōn*, which is translated as "rule" or "standard." In the ancient Greek world, this was the word for a measuring line, or what we might call a tape measure or ruler. In the New Testament, it is used in this sense twice. Galatians 6:16 uses it for an ethical/ theological "rule" of life, the rule of faith, as opposed to the rule of

Scripture, which included only an edited version of Luke's Gospel and ten of Paul's letters.[9] The believers spoke of the canon of Scripture as the only rule or measure of doctrine and life. For example, the great apologist of the ancient church, Irenaeus of Lyons, opposed a group known as the Gnostics when he said the Scriptures were "the Rule of the Truth."[10]

Against the canonical books of the Old and New Testaments, the Belgic Confession says, "Nothing can be alleged" (Art. 4). We believe these sixty-six books are distinguished from the apocryphal ("hidden") books, which the Roman Catholic and Eastern Orthodox churches consider to be inspired (BC, Art. 6). The apocryphal books are not divinely inspired "and therefore are of no authority in the Church of God, nor to be any otherwise approved, or made use of, than other human writings" (WCF, 1.3).

## AUTHORITY

That brings us back to the question of authority. The Belgic Confession goes on to say, "We receive all these books, and these only, as holy and canonical, for the regulation, foundation, and confirmation of our faith" (BC, Art. 5). Because the Word that God has given to us is inspired, it has an authority that demands that we "receive" it for what it is. We are creatures of the Creator, servants of the King. This means we are under His authority. Because of this, we must adjust our attitudes and begin to live with humility and reverence under the Lord. To do so, we must accept the Bible as God's revealed will for us.

Two primary evidences confirm the Scriptures as the Word of God to us. In the first place, "the Holy Ghost witnesseth in our hearts that they are from God" (BC, Art. 5). This witness of the Holy Spirit is the chief evidence for the Word of God. The Westminster Confession says of this work of the Holy Spirit: "our full persuasion and assurance of the infallible truth, and divine authority thereof, is from the inward work of the Holy Spirit bearing witness by and with the Word in our hearts" (1.5).

The second evidence is the self-authenticating nature of Scripture themselves. The Belgic Confession simply says, "They carry the evidence thereof in themselves," and because of this, "the very blind are able to perceive that the things foretold in them are fulfilling" (Art. 5). The Westminster Confession elaborates on the nature of Scripture by listing several characteristics that contribute to its self-authentication: ". . . the heavenliness of the matter, the efficacy of the doctrine, the majesty of the style, the consent of all the parts, the scope of the whole (which is to give all glory to God), the full discovery it makes of the only way of man's salvation, the many other incomparable excellencies, and the entire perfection thereof, are arguments whereby it doth abundantly evidence itself to be the Word of God" (1.5). In reading Scripture, we are lifted to heaven, convinced of its teaching, impressed by its style, led to see how it all

fits together, brought to give glory to God, and directed to Christ,
the way of salvation.

commented on this paragraph by saying that

marvellous knowledge it exhibits

relations and conditions; [and] in the original and luminous solution
it affords of many of the darkest problems of human history and
destiny."[11]

## SUFFICIENCY

We also believe in the sufficiency of the canonical Scriptures.
Regarding the sufficiency of the Word of God, Article 7 of the Belgic
Confession says that what we have in the Scriptures is enough for
us to be content as God's children. Echoing Peter, who said God's
"divine power has granted to us all things that pertain to life and
godliness, through the knowledge of him who called us to his own
glory and excellence" (2 Peter 1:3), the Belgic Confession speaks of
the sufficiency of the Word in terms of faith and the Christian life,
saying: "We believe that these Holy Scriptures fully contain the will
of God, and that whatsoever man ought to believe unto salvation,
is sufficiently taught therein. For . . . the whole manner of worship
which God requires of us is written in them at large" (Art. 7).

The Westminster Confession also defines the sufficiency of

Scripture in terms of the Christian's faith in God and the Christian life: "The whole counsel of God, concerning all things necessary for his own glory, man's salvation, faith, and life, is either expressly set down in Scripture, or by good and necessary consequence may be deduced from Scripture. . . . All things in Scripture are not alike plain in themselves, nor alike clear unto all; yet those things which are necessary to be known, believed, and observed, for salvation, are . . . clearly propounded and opened in some place of Scripture or other" (1.6, 7).

In fact, this sufficiency is so complete, we must not even begin to consider other writings, traditions, or men's interpretations as on the same level:

> Neither may we compare any writings of men, though ever so holy, with those divine Scriptures; nor ought we to compare custom, or the great multitude, or antiquity, or succession of times or persons, or councils, decrees, or statutes, with the truth of God, for the truth is above all: for all men are of themselves liars, and more vain than vanity itself. Therefore we reject with all our hearts whatsoever doth not agree with this infallible rule, which the Apostles have taught us, saying, *Try the spirits whether they are of God*; likewise, *If there come any unto you, and bring not this doctrine, receive him not into your house.* (BC, Art. 7)

## PERSPICUITY

Finally, this revelation from the infinite God to finite creatures that is His breathed-out words upon the canonical pages of the Old and New Testaments and that is authoritative and sufficient for our life in Christ is *perspicuous*. What does this word mean? It comes from the Latin word *perspicuitas*, meaning "clearness," and it simply tells

~~~led to us in letters, words, and con-

destruction" (2 Peter 3:16). Simply

is equally clear, and not everyone's understanding is the same. So what does it mean to say that Scripture is clear?

According to the Westminster Confession, biblical perspicuity pertains to the issue of salvation: "those things which are necessary to be known, believed, and observed for salvation, are so clearly propounded and opened in some place of Scripture or other, that not only the learned, but the unlearned, in a due use of the ordinary means, may attain unto a sufficient understanding of them" (1.7). Here is a wonderful promise for sinners, whether learned and educated with bachelor's, master's, or doctoral degrees, or with no degree at all except that which is earned through life. The promise is that anyone who uses "the ordinary means" of reading the Word, praying over the Word, and meditating on the Word can know the Lord: "Lord, to whom shall we go? You have the words of eternal life" (John 6:68).

## CONCLUSION

It is important to note that almost every evangelical Protestant church in our day would subscribe on paper to these statements about the

Word of God. But the real question is whether the confession that Scripture is God's inspired, canonical, authoritative, sufficient, and perspicuous revelation actually affects how Christians in any particular church practice their faith and live their lives. Simply stated, every church you may visit says, "We believe the Bible," but your response should be, "Show me."

In Reformed churches, we not only confess *sola Scriptura*, we seek to implement Scripture's authority in our worship in terms of what we do and why we do it. *Sola Scriptura* impacts our preaching as we allow Scripture to guide what we preach—choosing rich doctrines over hobby horses or "relevant" topics designed to draw in crowds. It affects our administration of the sacraments by revealing what we should regard as sacraments and by telling us how, when, and to whom we should administer them. It sets the standard for our exercise of godly church discipline. The list could go on.

This does not mean that we think we are perfect. But in all areas of church life, family life, and individual life, Reformed churches actively and wholeheartedly seek to bring all thoughts into captivity to Christ (2 Cor. 10:5) by means of Scripture, the final authority.

*Notes*

1  From the hymn "How Firm a Foundation" by John Rippon, 1787.

2  For a technical discussion of the development of the relationship between Scripture and tradition in the centuries leading up to the Reformation, see *Forerunners of the Reformation: The Shape of Late Medieval Thought Illustrated by Key Documents*, ed. Heiko A. Oberman, trans. Paul L. Nyhus (New York: Holt, Rinehart and Winston, 1966), 53–66.

3  For two excellent Reformation responses to the Council of Trent, see Martin Chemnitz, *Examination of the Council of Trent*, trans. Fred Kramer, 4 vols. (St.

Louis: Concordia Publishing House, 1978–1986), and John Calvin, *Canons and Decrees of the Council of Trent, with the Antidote* in *Selected Works of John Calvin:* ~~~ ed. Henry Beveridge and Jules Bonnet, 7 vols. (1858; repr.,

73–76.

6   On this doctrine, see *Sola Scriptura: The Protestant Position on ...* Kistler (1995; second ed., Orlando, Fla.: Reformation Trust, 2009).

7   J. I. Packer, *God Has Spoken: Revelation and the Bible* (1965; rev. ed., London: Hodder and Stoughton, 1979), 50.

8   On the history of the canon, see F. F. Bruce, *The Canon of Scripture* (Downers Grove, Ill.: InterVarsity Press, 1988). On the theological issues surrounding the canon from a Reformed perspective, see Herman N. Ridderbos, *Redemptive History and the New Testament Scriptures*, trans. H. De Jongste, rev. Richard B. Gaffin, Jr., Biblical & Theological Studies (1963; second rev. ed., Phillipsburg, N.J.: Presbyterian and Reformed, 1988).

9   For basic information about Marcion, see Louis Berkhof, *The History of Christian Doctrines* (1937; repr., Grand Rapids: Baker, 1990), 52–54; Henry Chadwick, *The Early Church* (1967; repr., New York: Penguin, 1990), 38–40, 80–81.

10  *St. Irenaeus of Lyons Against the Heresies: Volume 1: Book 1*, trans. Dominic J. Unger, rev. John J. Dillon, Ancient Christian Writers 55 (New York: Paulist Press, 1992), 48.

11  A. A. Hodge, *A Commentary on the Confession of Faith*, ed. W. H. Goold (London: T. Nelson and Sons, 1870), 36.

12  For an excellent introduction to this doctrine, see J. van Genderen and W. H. Velema, *Concise Reformed Dogmatics*, trans. Gerrit Bilkes and Ed M. van der Maas (Phillipsburg, N.J.: P&R, 2008), 96–101.

*Oh give thanks to the Lord; call upon his name;*
*Make known his deeds among the peoples!*

—Psalm 105:1

All scripts tell a story. They are designed to communicate the thoughts of an author on a particular subject to an audience. When we turn to the Scriptures as God's authoritative Word, we turn to His script.[1] His script tells a story, it is designed to communicate His thoughts, and it does so to an audience. As a script, the Word of God speaks of the mighty deeds of the Lord. The story that God communicates to us in the Scriptures has been famously described as "the greatest drama ever staged."[2]

So what is the Bible all about anyway? If you listen to surveys of what our culture thinks about the Bible or even listen to politically conservative talk-show hosts, you will conclude that the Bible is a book about how to be a good person and how to do unto others what you want them to do unto you. As a 2000 survey of American religious beliefs showed, seventy-five percent of Americans believe the Bible teaches that God helps those who help themselves.[3]

On the contrary, the Scriptures tell of God's wondrous deeds and thoughts toward us (Ps. 40:5). The Word of God traces the height, depth, and breadth of these deeds. We learn the dramatic story of how He created all things good (Gen. 1–2) and of how man turned all things bad by his sin, which we call "the fall" (Gen. 3). Yet God dramatically revealed Himself throughout the history of the Bible as the God of redemption (e.g., Gen. 3:15, 21) and as the One who one day would consummate His plan of redemption and bring His people and all that He had made into the condition He originally intended for them (Rev. 21–22).[4]

What unifies all the acts in the "greatest drama ever staged" is that they are expressed in the Bible through the concept of *covenant*.[5] A simple definition of a covenant is that it is a formal relationship between two parties that includes blessings and curses. As Zacharius Ursinus said, "A covenant in general is a mutual contract, or agreement between two parties, in which the one party binds itself to the other to accomplish some thing upon certain conditions, giving or receiving something, which is accompanied with certain outward signs and symbols, for the purpose of ratifying in the most solemn manner the contract entered into, and for the sake of confirming it, that the engagement may be kept inviolate."[6]

As we think of the story of Scripture through the concept of covenant, we need to recognize that while the Hebrew word for covenant, *berith*, is used two hundred and eighty-seven times in the Old Testament, reading the Bible through the lens of this concept has come to be a distinctive feature only of Reformed Protestantism. This is why some have said that Reformed theology is "covenant theology" and that to be Reformed is to be covenantal.[7] However, Reformed scholars have noted that the Bible was read this way by ˡ ᶠᵃᵗʰᵉʳˢ [8] As Augustine said:

pleases may read and know. ᴛ ᵘ. ᵉ made with the first man, is just this: "In the day ye eat thereof, ye shall surely die." Whence it is written in the book called Ecclesiasticus, "All flesh waxeth old as doth a garment. For the covenant from the beginning is, Thou shall die the death."[9]

In this chapter, I would like to trace the unfolding of God's covenants through what we might call the four major acts found in the Bible: creation, rebellion, redemption, and consummation.

## CREATION

The first act of God's story was creation. The Bible opens with this powerful statement: "In the beginning, God created the heavens and the earth" (Gen. 1:1). He created all things out of nothing (*ex nihilo*) and into nothing (*in nihilum*) by the word of His power (Gen. 1; cf. Ps. 33:6; John 1:1–3; Heb. 1:2–3), and He did so "in the space of six days" (WCF, 4.1). In the first three days, He created the *form* of all things, separating light from darkness (Gen. 1:4), the waters under the firmament from the waters above the firmament (Gen. 1:7), and the seas from the dry land (Gen. 1:9); in the second triad of days, He gave *fullness* to all He made: the sun for the day and the moon for the night (Gen. 1:16), creatures to fill the seas and air (Gen. 1:20), and creatures to fill the earth (Gen. 1:24).[10]

The high point of the creation week, though, was the creation of humanity on day six. God said, "Let us make man in our image, after our likeness" (Gen. 1:26). This meant, according to the psalmist, that man was "crowned . . . with glory and honor" (Ps. 8:5). The Heidelberg Catechism memorably explains the significance of Adam's creation, saying:

### Did God create man thus wicked and perverse?

No; but God created man good, and after his own image—that is, in righteousness and true holiness; that he might rightly know God his Creator, heartily love him, and live with him in eternal blessedness, to praise and glorify him. (Q&A 6)

God created the first man, Adam, in a covenant relationship with Himself (Gen. 2; cf. Hos. 6:7; Isa. 24:5). This covenant is variously called the *covenant of creation* because it was established at creation as a part of creation, the *covenant of nature* because it was a part of what man was by nature as an image-bearer of God, the *covenant of life* (WLC, Q&A 20; WSC, Q&A 12) because it was intended to give man not only earthly life but heavenly life, and the *covenant of works* (WCF, 7.2; WLC, Q&A 30) because this heavenly life was contingent on the basis of Adam's obedience to the law of the covenant. By means of this original covenant, "life was promised to Adam, and in him to his posterity, upon condition of perfect and personal obedience" (WCF, 7.2).

What exactly does this mean? As the Westminster Confession
‸ ‸ ‸‸‸‸ "the distance between God and the creature is
‸ ‸‸‸‸ fruition of Him as their

ment was, ⸤⸤⸤ ⸤⸤⸤⸥
tree of the knowledge of good and evil you ⸤⸤⸥
day that you eat of it you shall surely die" (Gen. 2:16–17). While the
commandment threatened eternal death, it implied the blessing of
eternal life that the old covenant law one day would express in these
words: "You shall therefore keep my statutes and my rules; if a person does them, he shall live by them: I am the LORD" (Lev. 18:5).
God put two trees in the Garden of Eden to signify His covenant in
a visible way. The tree of life signified not only earthly life, but also
the ultimate and eternal life that Adam was made to enjoy with God
(Gen. 2:9, 3:22; Rev. 2:7; 22:2, 14, 19). The tree of the knowledge of
good and evil signified God's law, with its stated penalty that Adam
would die in the day he ate thereof (Gen. 2:17).

The importance of understanding God's covenants in terms
of the distinction between the original covenant of works and the
subsequent covenant of grace (see below) was stated eloquently by
Wilhelmus à Brakel (1635–1711), an influential Dutch Reformed
minister and theologian, who said:

> We shall now speak of Adam as being in covenant with God—
> the covenant of works. Acquaintance with this covenant is of

the greatest importance, for whoever errs here or denies the existence of the covenant of works, will not understand the covenant of grace, and will readily err concerning the mediatorship of the Lord Jesus. Such a person will very readily deny that Christ by His active obedience has merited a right to eternal life for the elect. This is to be observed with several parties who, because they err concerning the covenant of grace, also deny the covenant of works. Conversely, whoever denies the covenant of works must rightly be suspected to be in error concerning the covenant of grace.[11]

## REBELLION

Although Adam was created in the image and likeness of God and was therefore "capable in all things to will agreeably to the will of God" (BC, Art. 14), he gave ear to the Devil, broke the terms of the original covenant, and fell under its sanction of death (Gen. 2:17), which was complete spiritual and physical death and separation from his God (Eph. 2:1). Therefore, "Man, by his fall . . . made himself incapable of life by that covenant" (WCF, 7.3). The Belgic Confession describes the rebellion of Adam, saying he "willfully subjected himself to sin and consequently to death and the curse, giving ear to the words of the devil. For the commandment of life, which he had received, he transgressed; and by sin separated himself from God, who was his true life" (Art. 14).

This tragic moment in the drama of Scripture had lasting effects on all humans, since Adam represented us all. Children in Colonial America used to learn this truth when they learned their alphabet in the *New England Primer*, when they said, "In Adam's fall, we sinned all." As Paul taught the church in Rome, because of the sin of the ... " ... because all sinned," meaning that

we pray with David, "Behold, I was brought ... sin did my mother conceive me" (Ps. 51:5). As the Canons of Dort confess, before his sin, Adam's "understanding was adorned with a true and saving knowledge of his Creator, and of spiritual things," but afterward he had "blindness of mind, horrible darkness, vanity, and perverseness of judgment"; before his sin, "his heart and will were upright," but afterward, he was "wicked, rebellious, and obdurate in heart and will"; before his sin, "all his affections [were] pure, and the whole Man was holy," but afterward, he was "impure in [all] his affections" (CD, 3/4.1). The canons go on to explain the bleakness of our condition: "Therefore all men are conceived in sin, and are by nature children of wrath, incapable of any saving good, prone to evil, dead in sin, and in bondage thereto; and, without the regenerating grace of the Holy Spirit, they are neither able nor willing to return to God, to reform the depravity of their nature, nor to dispose themselves to reformation" (CD, 3/4.3).

The great English preacher and poet John Donne (1572–1631) described the tragic results of Adam's rebellion and its effects on us in a poetic way in his "A Hymne to God the Father":

Wilt thou forgive that sinne where I begunne,
Which was my sin, though it were done before?
Wilt thou forgive that sinne; through which I runne,
And do run still: though still I do deplore?
When thou hast done, thou hast not done,
For I have more.[13]


## REDEMPTION

The rebellion of humanity was tragic. Yet after chronicling our resulting sinful state (Eph. 2:1–3), the apostle Paul said, "But God . . ." (v. 4). These two little words highlight the amazing contrast between our sin and God's grace. At the moment of Adam's fall, God began to show His mercy in withholding immediate physical death and to show His grace in promising to send another to redeem fallen humanity from its plight (Gen. 3:15). With this promise, in His amazing grace, God preached the "first gospel," which Christian theologians have called the *protoeuangelion*, or the "mother promise" (Dutch, *moederbelofte*), because from it come all others. The entire drama of Scripture from this point forward is the story of how God revealed this grace by initiating a new covenant to replace the one Adam had violated: ". . . the Lord was pleased to make a second [covenant], commonly called the covenant of grace; wherein he freely offered unto sinners life and salvation by Jesus Christ, requiring of them faith in him that they may be saved, and promising to give unto all those that are ordained unto eternal life, his Holy Spirit, to make them willing and able to believe" (WCF, 7.3).

## The Covenant of Grace

Reformed Christians speak of Scripture as the unfolding drama
~~ ~~ ~~~~ ~~ grace. We do this because the apostle Paul
~~

has varied by time and place. ~ ~~
widened from the Old Testament to the New Testament, as it was
administered first with small families (e.g., the families of Noah and
Abram), then with the nation of Israel, but now with the church,
which is made up of people "from every tribe and language and
people and nation" (Rev. 5:9). Also, it was administered in the Old
Testament through what the New Testament authors describe as
"types" and "shadows" (Heb. 8:5; 10:1), such as sacrifices, the priesthood, and the temple, all of which pointed to their reality, Jesus
Christ (e.g., Col. 2:17).

The Reformed creeds and confessions express the continuity
of God's covenant of grace despite its many historical variations.
For instance, the Heidelberg Catechism says: ". . . God himself first
revealed [it] in Paradise, [and] afterwards [it was] proclaimed by the
holy Patriarchs and Prophets, and foreshadowed by the sacrifices and
other ceremonies of the law, and finally fulfilled in his well-beloved
Son" (Q&A 19). This means the Bible is one story of the gospel,
which God has spoken "in many times and in many ways" (Heb.
1:1), whether in Paradise to Adam; during the days of the patriarchs,

such as Noah, Abraham, Isaac, Jacob, and Moses; through the ministry of the prophets, such as Isaiah, Jeremiah, Hosea, and Joel; or through the ceremonies of the Levitical sacrifices. All of this came to fruition in Jesus Christ.

Likewise, while recognizing the variations in the administration of the covenant of grace between the Old and New Testaments, the Westminster Confession of Faith affirms the continuity of the covenant in the promise of Christ and His fulfillment of it:

> This covenant was differently administered in the time of the law and in the time of the gospel: under the law it was administered by promises, prophecies, sacrifices, circumcision, the paschal lamb, and other types and ordinances delivered to the people of the Jews, all fore-signifying Christ to come, which were for that time sufficient and efficacious, through the operation of the Spirit, to instruct and build up the elect in faith in the promised Messiah, by whom they had full remission of sins, and eternal salvation; and is called the Old Testament.
>
> Under the gospel, when Christ the substance was exhibited, the ordinances in which this covenant is dispensed are the preaching of the word and the administration of the sacraments of Baptism and the Lord's Supper; which, though fewer in number, and administered with more simplicity and less outward glory, yet in them, it is held forth in more fullness, evidence, and spiritual efficacy, to all nations, both Jews and Gentiles; and is called the New Testament. There are not, therefore, two covenants of grace differing in substance, but one and the same under various dispensations. (7.5–6)

When our Lord Jesus Christ was born, lived, died, and was raised from the grave, the covenant of grace reached its zenith in what the ～、、 ᵘ ᵗʰᵉ ᵖᵉʷ ᶜᵒᵛᵉⁿᵃⁿᵗ" (Jer. 31:31; Luke 22:20; 1 Cor. 11:25;

He, our Savior, has ᵗᵒ～～ᵉᵌ
Set us free from dire distress.
Through His merit we inherit
Light and peace and happiness.[14]

### The Covenant of Redemption

Standing behind these two great covenants in history, the covenant of works before the fall and the covenant of grace after the fall, is yet another, the covenant of redemption.[15] From all of eternity, even before there was a covenant of works or a covenant of grace, God the Father, God the Son, and God the Holy Spirit covenanted to share Their eternal love and fellowship with Their creatures. In human terms, God the Father covenanted to create a people, whom He knew would sin; to choose from this fallen mass "a great multitude that no one could number" (Rev. 7:9); and to give them to Christ (John 17:24), whom He would "crush" on the cross according to His eternal will (Isa. 53:10). The Son covenanted to accomplish their redemption: "I glorified you on earth, having accomplished the work that you gave me to do" (John 17:4). The Holy Spirit covenanted to apply the work of the Son to those the Father chose, "until we acquire possession of it" (Eph. 1:14).

This covenant of redemption among the members of the Holy Trinity opens up to us the biblical doctrine of predestination. When the Bible speaks of those the Father gave to the Son to receive grace and glory, it speaks of election. Although there is much misunderstanding and mystery surrounding this doctrine, the Reformed churches believe that our approach to it needs to be that of the apostle Paul. Paul did not reject it but praised God for it, saying, "Blessed be the God and Father of our Lord Jesus Christ, who has blessed us in Christ with every spiritual blessing in the heavenly places, even as he chose us in him before the foundation of the world, that we should be holy and blameless before him" (Eph. 1:3–4).

There are a couple of key points to note about election to salvation. First, election was "from the foundation of the world," that is, from all of eternity. It was not an afterthought in God's mind, but was always His purpose for His people. Second, election is unchangeable (CD, 1.11). The number of those chosen for salvation cannot be increased or decreased. When Paul penned what theologians call the "golden chain of salvation," he expressed this certainty: "For those whom he foreknew he also predestined to be conformed to the image of his Son, in order that he might be the firstborn among many brothers. And those whom he predestined he also called, and those whom he called he also justified, and those whom he justified he also glorified" (Rom. 8:29–30). Third, election was according to the sovereign power and good pleasure of God alone (CD, 1.10). He did not choose because He saw anyone choosing Him first. This is what Paul teaches when he says of Jacob and Esau, Moses and Pharaoh:

Though [Jacob and Esau] were not yet born and had done nothing either good or bad—in order that God's purpose of election might continue, not because of works but because of him who calls—[Rebekah] was told, "The older ⸱ll ⸱⸱⸱⸱⸱⸱ the younger." As it is written, "Jacob I loved, but

raised you up, that I might ⸱⸱⸱⸱ ⸱⸱⸱ ⸱⸱⸱ ⸱ ⸱ my name might be proclaimed in all the earth." So then he has mercy on whomever he wills, and he hardens whomever he wills. (Rom. 9:11–18)

When the Reformed churches gathered at the Synod of Dort, they summarized the biblical doctrine of election, saying, "Election is the unchangeable purpose of God, whereby, before the foundation of the world, He has out of mere grace, according to the sovereign good pleasure of His own will, chosen from the whole human race, which had fallen through their own fault from their primitive state of uprightness into sin and destruction, a certain number of persons to redemption in Christ, whom He from eternity appointed the Mediator and Head of the elect and the foundation of salvation" (CD, 1.7).

Related to election is its opposite, what theologians call "reprobation." In the covenant of redemption, God the Father gave to the Son a people to redeem and to call to faith by the Holy Spirit. Yet He did not give all humanity to His Son to be saved. Some were designated to be rescued from sin while others were left in their sinful state. These God passed by and in His justice left "in the common misery into which they have willfully plunged themselves . . . permitting them in His just judgment to follow their own ways" (CD, 1.15). While Jacob was loved by God, Esau was hated (Rom. 9:13). While Moses was a recipient of mercy, Pharaoh's heart was hardened (Rom. 9:15–18). While believers are called "a chosen race, a royal priesthood, a holy nation, a people for [God's] own possession" (1 Peter 2:9), unbelievers are said to have rejected and stumbled over Christ: "They stumble because they disobey the word, as they were destined to do" (1 Peter 2:4, 7, 8).

We should be humbled by the sins we have committed that deserve just punishment so that God may be exalted for the grace that has freed us from His punishment. As Paul says: "But who are you, O man, to answer back to God? Will what is molded say to its molder, 'Why have you made me like this?'" (Rom. 9:20). Then we may rejoice with Paul: "Oh, the depth of the riches and wisdom and knowledge of God! How unsearchable are his judgments and how inscrutable his ways! 'For who has known the mind of the Lord, or who has been his counselor?' Or 'who has given a gift to him that he might be repaid?' For from him and through him and to him are all things. To him be glory forever. Amen" (Rom. 11:33–36).

## CONSUMMATION

The fourth and final act of the dramatic unfolding of God's covenant is in what we call the consummation, in which, at the end of all things, God will "unite all things in [Christ], things in heaven and things on earth" (Eph. 1:10).

Several things will happen to bring God's purposes to completion.[16] First, our Lord Jesus Christ will return "when the time appointed by the Lord (which is unknown to all creatures) is come,

~~…………… of the elect complete,"~~ at which time Christ "will

the Lord in the air, and so we will ……… 4:16–17).

Second, as the verse just above notes, Jesus will raise up the dead (John 5:28–29; 6:40). When He does that, "their souls [will be] joined and united with their proper bodies in which they formerly lived" (BC, Art. 37). In particular, He will transform His redeemed people's bodies to be fit vessels to dwell with Him in eternity (Rom. 8:23; 1 Cor. 15:35–58).

Third, Jesus will "judge the living and the dead" (Apostles' Creed). He will summon all humanity before His judgment throne, open the books, and judge all for what they have done in this world. This judgment will reveal two attributes of God's nature: "The end of God's appointing this day, is for the manifestation of the glory of his mercy in the eternal salvation of the elect; and of his justice in the damnation of the reprobate, who are wicked and disobedient" (WCF, 33.2). It also will provoke a twofold attitude in humanity, as the Belgic Confession says: "The consideration of this judgment is justly terrible and dreadful to the wicked and ungodly, but most desirable and comfortable to the righteous and the elect" (Art. 37).

The Second Coming of Christ is comforting to those who embrace

Jesus Christ, not condemning, because Christians shall experience the mercy of God on that day. The Reformed confessions speak of this great comfort:

> [T]heir full deliverance shall be perfected, and there they shall receive the fruits of their labor and trouble which they have borne . . . the faithful and elect shall be crowned with glory and honor; and the Son of God will confess their names before God his Father, and his elect angels; all tears shall be wiped from their eyes; and their cause, which is now condemned by many judges and magistrates as heretical and impious, will then be known to be the cause of the Son of God. And, for a gracious reward, the Lord will cause them to possess such a glory as never entered into the heart of man to conceive. (BC, Art. 37)

### What comfort is it to thee that Christ shall come again to judge the quick and the dead?

That in all my sorrows and persecutions, with uplifted head, I look for the self-same One who has before offered himself for me to the judgment of God, and removed from me all curse, to come again as Judge from heaven; who shall cast all his and my enemies into everlasting condemnation, but shall take me, with all his chosen ones, to himself, into heavenly joy and glory. (HC, Q&A 52)

Fourth, there will be a renewal of creation. Jesus described the consummation of all things as "the regeneration" (Matt. 19:28, NASB), since He will give this world a new birth. Peter preached an early sermon in the life of the church calling the end the "restoration of all things" (Acts 3:21, NASB). The Belgic Confession

· ·1· ·1 ·· ··· ·· ··· our Lord will burn "this old world with

21–22), wherein ·················
age will be so glorious, Paul says all creation "waits with eager longing" to be "set free from its bondage to corruption" (Rom. 8:19, 21). For Christians, it is "in this hope we were saved" (Rom. 8:24), which means that the return of Christ and all He will bring is our "blessed hope" (Titus 2:13). This cosmic dimension of the work of Christ that will consummate all things was expressed by the apostle Paul when he said "all things were created through him and for him," and that through Christ, God will "reconcile to himself all things, whether on earth or in heaven" (Col. 1:16, 20).

This final state will be greater than that which Adam and Eve experienced in the Garden of Eden. As Paul says, "What no eye has seen, nor ear heard, nor the heart of man imagined . . . God has prepared for those who love him" (1 Cor. 2:9). With these glorious truths in mind, Reformed believers "expect that great day with a most ardent desire, to the end that we may fully enjoy the promises of God in Christ Jesus our Lord. Amen" (BC, Art. 37). It is for that Day that we must join the church, ever praying, *Maranatha*, "Our Lord, come!" (1 Cor. 16:22), and, "Amen. Come, Lord Jesus!" (Rev. 22:20).

## CONCLUSION

This story of creation, rebellion, redemption, and consummation is the script that is played out so dramatically throughout Scripture, from the beginning of creation in the book of Genesis to the glorious consummation in the book of Revelation. In between are all the twists and turns of humanity's rebellion against their Creator. Yet their Creator is also their Redeemer, who, despite His people's constant sin and rebellion, has accomplished His plan of redemption in Christ and will consummate it in eternity—"to the praise of his glorious grace" (Eph. 1:6).

*Notes*

1   On the idea of a script as a metaphor for God's Word, see Michael S. Horton, *Covenant and Eschatology: The Divine Drama* (Louisville: Westminster John Knox, 2002); Kevin J. Vanhoozer, *The Drama of Doctrine: A Canonical-Linguistic Approach to Christian Theology* (Louisville: Westminster John Knox, 2005).

2   This is the title of a famous essay by Dorothy Sayers, "The Greatest Drama Ever Staged Is the Official Creed of Christendom," in *The Whimsical Christian: 18 Essays by Dorothy L. Sayers* (New York: Macmillan, 1978), 11–16.

3   http://www.theologicalstudies.citymax.com/page/page/1572910.htm (accessed May 16, 2009).

4   For a great article that gives an overview of the entire Bible, see R. Scott Clark, "What the Bible is All About," *Modern Reformation* 16:2 (March/April 2007): 20–24.

5   For a classic Reformed exposition of covenant theology, see Herman Witsius, *The Economy of the Covenants Between God and Man: Comprehending a Complete Body of Divinity*, trans. William Crookshank, 2 vols. (1822; repr., Phillipsburg, N.J.: P&R, 1990). For two recent presentations, see O. Palmer Robertson, *The Christ of the Covenants* (Phillipsburg, N.J.: P&R, 1980), and Michael Horton, *God of Promise: Introducing Covenant Theology* (Grand Rapids: Baker, 2006).

6   Zacharius Ursinus, *Commentary on the Heidelberg Catechism*, trans. George Willard (1852; repr., Phillipsburg, N.J.: P&R, 1985), 97.

7   I. John Hesselink, *On Being Reformed* (New York: Reformed Church Press, 1988), 55; cf. Steven M. Baugh, "Covenant Theology Illustrated: Romans 5 on the Federal Headship of Adam and Christ," *Modern Reformation* 9:4 (July/August 2000): 16–23.

. . . . . . . . *Anto-Nicene Theology* (Ph.D. diss.,

12  For an in-depth exegesis of this passage, see John Murray, *The Imputation of Adam's Sin* (1959; repr., Phillipsburg, N.J.: Presbyterian and Reformed, 1977).

13  John Donne, "A Hymne to God the Father," in *The Works of John Donne* (Hertfordshire, England: Wordsworth Editions, 1994), 187.

14  "Praise the Savior," in *Psalter Hymnal* (Grand Rapids: Christian Reformed Church, 1976), #361.

15  On this covenant, see Herman Bavinck, *Reformed Dogmatics, Vol. 3: Sin and Salvation in Christ*, ed. John Bolt, trans. John Vriend (Grand Rapids: Baker Academic, 2006), 212–216; M. J. Bosma, *Exposition of Reformed Doctrine* (1907; fourth ed., Grand Rapids: Smitter, 1927), 119–125.

16  For contemporary Reformed expositions of eschatology, see Kim Riddlebarger, *A Case for Amillennialism: Understanding the End Times* (Grand Rapids: Baker, 2003), and Cornelis P. Venema, *The Promise of the Future* (Edinburgh: Banner of Truth, 2000). This last book has recently been released in a shorter, more popular format, titled *Christ and the Future: The Bible's Teaching About the Last Things* (Edinburgh: Banner of Truth, 2008).

*Indeed, I count everything as loss because of the*
*surpassing worth of knowing Christ Jesus my Lord.*
*For his sake I have suffered the loss of all things and*
*count them as rubbish, in order that I may gain Christ*
*and be found in him, not having a righteousness of my*
*own that comes from the law, but that which comes*
*through faith in Christ, the righteousness from God*
*that depends on faith.*

—Philippians 3:8–9

**A**ction! Every script is intended to be used by the actors and actresses to play their parts in the story. As we have seen, as the inspired and authoritative Word of God to man, the Scriptures of the Old and New Testaments are the script, so to speak, of Christianity. This script describes the broad outlines of God's story in the unfolding of God's covenant relationship with Adam in the garden, Adam's violation of that covenant, and God's subsequent establishment of another covenant.

Since we are the sons and daughters of Adam, and therefore sinful like him, we need to ask how we personally come to participate in this new covenant of grace that God established. After all, God is "holy, holy, holy" (Isa. 6:3) and is "of purer eyes than to behold evil, and cannot look on wickedness" (Hab. 1:13, NKJV). Because of this, the prophet Nahum asked, "Who can stand before his indignation? Who can endure the heat of his anger?" (Nah. 1:6), and Job cried out, "How can a man be righteous before God?" (Job 9:2, NKJV). What we learn through the concept of covenant is that the central teaching of Scripture is how this offended and holy God *Himself* provides a means of redemption and reconciliation so that fallen and sinful human beings can have a relationship with Him. This central teaching of how sinners can stand before a holy God is called "justification" in Scripture (Rom. 4:25; 5:16, 18).[1]

In this chapter, I want to explore what the Bible teaches about justification—that it is by God's *grace alone*, received by us through *faith alone*, which is placed in *Christ alone*. In justification, God forgives all our sins and declares us righteous in His sight. Because of this, He enters into a relationship with us whereby we cry out, "Abba! Father!" (Gal. 4:6). Our Reformed forefathers called this doctrine the "material cause" of the Protestant Reformation. The question of authority was the "formal," or foundational, cause of the Reformation, and once it was answered, the Reformers found in the Scriptures the "material" to answer the question of how a sinner can be right with God.

## THE WEAKNESS OF THE LAW

...because we cannot save our-

curse, man can ...

This article lists three reasons why obedience...
justify us. First, while the law shows us our sins and convicts us, it
does not contain the remedy for those sins. As Paul says: "Now we
know that whatever the law says it speaks to those who are under
the law, so that every mouth may be stopped, and the whole world
may be held accountable to God. For by works of the law no human
being will be justified in his sight, since through the law comes
knowledge of sin" (Rom. 3:19–20).

Second, the law does not give us the strength to get ourselves
out of our miserable condition. Instead of increasing our abilities,
Paul says, "the law came in to increase the trespass" (Rom. 5:20).
He goes on to say that "while we were living in the flesh, our sinful passions, aroused by the law, were at work in our members
to bear fruit for death" (Rom. 7:5). The powerlessness of the law
is seen even more strikingly when Paul says: "But sin, seizing an
opportunity through the commandment, produced in me all kinds
of covetousness. For apart from the law, sin lies dead. I was once
alive apart from the law, but when the commandment came, sin
came alive and I died. The very commandment that promised life

proved to be death to me. For sin, seizing an opportunity through the commandment, deceived me and through it killed me" (Rom. 7:8–11).

Third, the law is weakened through the flesh. This means that because of our sinful nature, the problem is not the law, but us. In a blame-shifting culture such as ours, there is no one to blame but ourselves: "For we know that the law is spiritual, but I am of the flesh, sold under sin. . . . For God has done what the law, weakened by the flesh, could not do" (Rom. 7:14; 8:3). All we can do is cry out, "Have mercy on me, O God" (Ps. 51:1).

## JUSTIFICATION: JUST THE FACTS

So what are the basic facts about the concept of justification? The Heidelberg Catechism cuts through any double-talk and all man-made tradition when it simply asks the most profound question we can ask: "How are you righteous before God?" (Q&A 60). This question gets at the heart of what Reformed churches are all about, what the Bible is all about, and what our human condition before God is all about. The catechism answers this question by saying:

> Only by true faith in Jesus Christ; that is, though my conscience accuse me that I have grievously sinned against all the commandments of God, and have never kept any of them, and that I am still prone always to all evil, yet God, without any merit of mine, of mere grace, grants and imputes to me the perfect satisfaction, righteousness, and holiness of Christ, as if I had never committed nor had any sin, and had myself accomplished all the obedience which

Christ has rendered for me, if only I accept such benefit with a believing heart.

Catechism. I remember the first time I heard
ogy professor in college recite it before us in class. I was changed forever. It was the first time in my young Christian life I had ever heard of justification. I immediately returned to my dorm, typed out the words, printed it out, hung it on the wall above my desk, and proceeded to memorize it. This answer brought much clarity to my mind concerning my salvation and purpose to my heart concerning my reason for worshiping God for what His Son had done for me:

### What is justification?

Justification is an act of God's free grace unto sinners, in which he pardoneth all their sins, accepteth and accounteth their persons righteous in his sight; not for any thing wrought in them, or done by them, but only for the perfect obedience and full satisfaction of Christ, by God imputed to them, and received by faith alone. (Q&A 70)

"Free grace . . . received by faith alone . . . only for the perfect obedience and full satisfaction of Christ." There is the gospel in a nutshell. Isn't it beautiful?

## GRACE ALONE

Let us think about each of the aspects of justification one by one. In meditating on each, we will come to appreciate our salvation even more and be led to worship with more passion.

### *The Backstory*

Every story has a backstory, the background facts. Before we even think about God justifying us by grace alone, we have to ask ourselves, How could an offended God reconcile Himself with those who had offended Him? As we have seen, after God made Adam "very good" in His image and likeness (Gen. 1:26–27, 31), Adam was "capable in all things to will agreeably to the will of God" (BC, Art. 14). Despite being able to do what God had commanded him, namely, "Of the tree of the knowledge of good and evil you shall not eat" (Gen. 2:17), he willfully and rebelliously sinned against God and brought on himself God's curse—physical and spiritual death. Because of Adam's sin, this penalty, known as "original sin," is "extended to all mankind" (BC, Art. 15). Therefore, we are born sinful (Ps. 51:5). As Jesus says, we are slaves of sin (John 8:34), and as Paul says, we are at war with God (Rom. 8:5–8).

With this backstory in mind, we need to ask, what is grace? Grace is God's favorable disposition toward us. It is *unmerited favor* because we have done nothing to deserve it. The Heidelberg Catechism says we have never kept any of the commandments of God. In fact, God is gracious toward us despite our having sinned against Him in every way possible. He saves despite "my conscience accus[ing] me that I have grievously sinned against all the commandments of God" (HC, Q&A 60).

Now you know why Paul expresses wonder over God's grace in saving *us*, who deserve nothing and who have forfeited all hope of eternal life, when he says, "But God, being rich in mercy, because of the great love with which he loved us, even when we were dead in our trespasses, made us alive together with Christ—by grace you have been saved" (Eph 2:4–5). He also describes God's grace by means of an employer-employee metaphor: "Now to the one who works, his wages are not counted as a gift but as his due. And to the one who does not work but believes in him who justifies the ungodly, his faith is counted as righteousness" (Rom. 4:4–5). As the King James Version translates this passage, the wages of the worker are given not by "grace" but by "debt." How wonderful it is that God does not account our salvation the same way, for we could never do enough.

### *Justification by Grace*

Justification is the result of God's grace *alone*. It can be no other way. As the Scriptures say: "For by grace you have been saved through faith. And this is not your own doing; it is the gift of God, not a result of works, so that no one may boast" (Eph. 2:8–9). Here Paul contrasts "grace" with "your own doing" and "gift" with "works" to point out the divine initiative in salvation. He continues elsewhere, saying, "All have sinned and fall short of the glory of God, and are justified by his grace as a gift, through the redemption that is in Christ Jesus (Rom. 3:23–24). Other passages that connect the grace of God to our justification abound:

> In him we have redemption through his blood, the forgiveness of our trespasses, according to the riches of his grace. (Eph. 1:7)

. . . share in suffering for the gospel by the power of God, who saved us and called us to a holy calling, not because of our works but because of his own purpose and grace, which he gave us in Christ Jesus before the ages began, and which now has been manifested through the appearing of our Savior Christ Jesus, who abolished death and brought life and immortality to light through the gospel. (2 Tim. 1:8–10)

. . . so that being justified by his grace we might become heirs according to the hope of eternal life. (Titus 3:7)

The Heidelberg Catechism succinctly confesses this truth, saying, "Yet God . . . of mere grace" (Q&A 60) saves us, while the Westminster Larger Catechism says simply, "Justification is an act of God's free grace" (Q&A 70). Question and answer 71 of the Larger Catechism marvelously goes on to exposit the meaning of grace alone (*sola gratia*), saying:

### How is justification an act of God's free grace?

Although Christ, by his obedience and death, did make a proper, real, and full satisfaction to God's justice in the behalf of them that are justified; yet in as much as God accepteth the satisfaction from a surety, which he might have demanded of them, and did provide this surety, his own only Son, imputing his righteousness to them, and requiring nothing of them for their justification but faith, which also is his gift, their justification is to them of free grace.

There are four reasons why justification is by grace alone, according to the Larger Catechism: first, God accepted Christ's satisfaction; second, God provided Christ; third, God imputes to us Christ's righteousness; and fourth, God requires nothing of us but faith, which is His gift to us:

> Amazing grace! how sweet the sound,
> That saved a wretch like *me*!
> I once was lost, but now am found,
> Was blind, but now I see.[3]

## FAITH ALONE

The only means by which sinners receive this grace of God so that they can be justified is faith. In order to make Christ's work our work, we must have faith in Christ.

### *The Holy Spirit*

We cannot believe in Christ and receive grace in our naturally sinful state. We first need the sovereign Holy Spirit to give us new birth (John 3:1–8). Because of this, we confess "the Holy Ghost kindleth in our hearts an upright faith, which embraces Jesus Christ with all His merits, appropriates Him, and seeks nothing more besides Him" (BC, Art. 22). This is what Paul meant when he said it is "by grace" that we are saved and that it is "through faith."

Furthermore, this faith "is the gift of God" (Eph. 2:8–9). As Paul says elsewhere: "It has been granted to you that for the sake of Christ you should . . . believe in him" (Phil. 1:29). Our justification is so much by grace alone that even the means by which we receive it is given to us by the grace of God. The Canons of Dort explain that faith is not regarded as a gift "on account of its being offered by God to man, to be accepted or rejected at his pleasure." Neither is it a gift "because it is in reality conferred, breathed, and infused into him; nor even because God bestows the power or ability to believe, and then expects that man should, by the exercise of his own free will, consent to the terms of salvation, and actually believe in Christ." Rather, it is a gift "because he who works in man both to will and to do, and indeed all things in all, produces both the will to believe and the act of believing also" (CD, 3/4.14).

## *Without Works*

Because we receive Christ by the faith that the Holy Spirit gives us, we "say with Paul, that we *are justified by faith* alone, or *by faith without works*" (BC, Art. 22). This is the language of Scripture. For example, Paul says of the gospel of Jesus Christ, "in it the righteousness of God is revealed from faith for faith, as it is written, 'The righteous shall live by faith'" (Rom. 1:17; cf. Hab. 2:4). This faith is contrasted with works throughout the New Testament to clearly teach us that justification is God's work, not ours. For instance: "But now the righteousness of God has been manifested apart from the law . . . the righteousness of God through faith in Jesus Christ . . . whom God put forward as a propitiation by his blood, to be received by faith . . . so that he might be just and the justifier of the one who has faith in Jesus" (Rom. 3:21, 22, 25, 26).

It is important to note that *faith itself* does not justify us. Contrary to popular expression, we do not believe we are saved *by faith*. We believe we are saved by God's *grace* and that our faith, being a gift of God, "is only an instrument with which we embrace Christ our Righteousness. But Jesus Christ, imputing to us all his merits, and so many holy works, which he hath done for us and in our stead, is our Righteousness. And faith is an instrument that keeps us in communion with him in all his benefits, which, when they become ours, are more than sufficient to acquit us of our sins" (BC, Art. 22).

To say that we are justified by faith in some way was a teaching of the early seventeenth century that the Reformed churches rejected at the Synod of Dort. Some taught that justification was not by a faith that accepted Christ, but "that God, having revoked the demand of perfect obedience of faith, regards faith itself and the obedience of faith, although imperfect, as the perfect obedience of the law, and does esteem it worthy of the reward of eternal life through grace" (CD, 2, Rejection of Errors 4). Our Reformed forefathers cited Romans 3:24–25 and said these teachers proclaimed "a new and strange justification of man before God, against the consensus of the whole church" (CD, 2, Rejection of Errors 4).

To summarize all the above, we might simply turn to the Westminster Confession of Faith, which describes justifying faith as a "receiving and resting on [Christ] and his righteousness" (11.1, 2). This means that faith is only as good as the object in which it rests—which, for the Christian, is Jesus Christ the righteous Savior.

## CHRIST ALONE

Thus, the only basis upon which God in His grace can accept sinners is the work of His Son, Jesus Christ.[4] Because of our natural and actual sin, and our total inability to save ourselves, God had to act dramatically and come to the rescue in the person and work of Jesus. As the Belgic Confession says so beautifully, it was "out of mere and perfect love" that God "sent his Son to assume that nature in which the disobedience was committed, to make satisfaction in the same, and to bear the punishment of sin by his most bitter passion and death" (BC, Art. 20).

This grace and love of God was stated most memorably in the words of Jesus Himself, who spoke of the reason why His Father sent Him: "For God so loved the world, that he gave his only Son, that whoever believes in him should not perish but have eternal life" (John 3:16).

The work that our Lord Jesus Christ accomplished has been helpfully distinguished by our Reformed forefathers into His active and passive obedience.

### *Active Obedience*

Christ's active obedience is His obedience to the law of God in thought, word, and deed from the moment of His conception through the end of His earthly life. The Heidelberg Catechism speaks memorably of Christ's active obedience when it says His "perfect satisfaction, righteousness, and holiness" become our own by faith alone (Q&A 61). The Westminster Larger Catechism also gives great attention to the lifelong obedience of our Lord on our behalf:

> **How did Christ humble himself in his life?**
> Christ humbled himself in his life, by subjecting himself to the law, which he perfectly fulfilled; and by conflicting with the indignities of the world, temptations of Satan, and infirmities in his flesh, whether common to the nature of man, or particularly accompanying that his low condition. (Q&A 48)

This also is how the apostle Paul explained our justification, saying: "Therefore, as one trespass led to condemnation for all men, so one act of righteousness leads to justification and life for all men. For as by the one man's disobedience the many were made sinners, so by the one man's obedience the many will be made righteous" (Rom. 5:18–19).

The truth that the righteousness of Jesus Christ alone is the foundation for our justification has profound practical effects in us, such as peace of conscience from the terrible judgment of God (Rom. 5:1). The apostle Paul's desire for the benefits of justification was so strong that he described his intense desire to "be found in him [Christ], not having a righteousness of my own that comes from the law, but that which comes through faith in Christ, the righteousness from God that depends on faith" (Phil. 3:9).

### *Passive Obedience*

When we speak of our Lord's passive obedience, we do not mean that He passively allowed things to happen to Him. Instead, we are speaking of His passion. The Latin word *passio* speaks of His sufferings on our behalf. Again, the Heidelberg Catechism is very helpful, because it tells us the passive obedience of Christ has to do not merely with His death but with His entire life:

> **What dost thou understand by the word *Suffered*?**
> That all the time he lived on earth, but especially at the end of his life, he bore, in body and soul, the wrath of God against the sin of the whole human race, in order that by his passion, as the only atoning sacrifice, he might redeem our body and soul from everlasting damnation, and obtain

for us the grace of God, righteousness, and eternal life. (Q&A 37)

Because of our gratitude for the work of Jesus Christ alone in both His active and passive obedience, which culminated in His once-for-all accomplishment on the cross for us, we desire "to know nothing . . . except Jesus Christ and him crucified" (1 Cor. 2:2), and we "count everything as loss because of the surpassing worth of knowing Christ Jesus" (Phil. 3:8).

### Satisfaction

This obedience of Christ, especially His sufferings, made a full satisfaction of the justice of God. What does this mean? Since God is a supremely just God, sinners must be punished with temporal and eternal punishment both in body and soul. Since all human beings are sinners, none of us can escape this punishment unless we satisfy the justice of God (CD, 2.1). This is why God gave Jesus to us. He did what we cannot do, "becoming a curse for us" on the cross (Gal. 3:13; CD, 2.2). Christ's death, then, actually satisfied God's justice. It did not just make this satisfaction possible, it actually accomplished it once for all, for all those the Lord intended to save.

While Jesus' death was "abundantly sufficient to expiate the sins of the whole world" (CD, 2.3), its efficiency—that is, its power and accomplishment—were offered on behalf of those the Father had given Him from all eternity. While this doctrine was called "limited atonement" by the Arminians as a political way of cornering the Reformed churches, the Reformed have spoken of the death of Christ as both sufficient and efficient. It is able to save a thousand worlds full of sinners, but it actually saved those God intended to save.

## *Imputation*

One last word about justification is necessary. Not only do Reformed Christians teach that we are justified by God's grace alone, through faith alone, in Christ alone, we also insist on the method by which Christ's righteousness is given to us: imputation.

In contrast with the Roman Catholic Church's teaching that justification occurs when God's grace is infused into sinners, who then cooperate with this grace to make themselves holy, the Reformers taught that God imputes Christ's righteousness to sinners. To impute is to credit. God credits Christ's righteousness to us, and it becomes ours.

While most modern Bible translations use the term *reckon* or *credit*, the classic language of imputation can be seen in Paul's teaching on justification in Romans 4 in the King James Version. After discussing the biblical teaching that Abraham was not justified through works but through faith (Rom. 4:1–3), Paul quotes from Psalm 32: "Even as David also describeth the blessedness of the man, unto whom God imputeth righteousness without works, saying, Blessed are they whose iniquities are forgiven, and whose sins are covered. Blessed is the man to whom the Lord will not impute sin" (Rom. 4:6–8, KJV). Furthermore, Paul says, Abraham was justified before he was circumcised, "that he might be the father of all them that believe, though they be not circumcised; that righteousness might be imputed unto them also" (Rom. 4:11, KJV). He drives home the benefit of this for us when he goes on to say, "Now it was not written for his sake alone, that it was imputed to him; but for us also, to whom it shall be imputed, if we believe on him that raised up Jesus our Lord from the dead" (Rom. 4:23–24, KJV). The imputation of Christ's righteousness is vitally important because it guards the graciousness of our salvation, apart from any and all works.

## CONCLUSION

Expressing the amazing truth that our holy God justifies sinners is the purpose of the narrative of God's redemptive drama. What a drama it is. The eternal God, who created us so freely, in such blessedness, and whom we rejected in the garden so ungratefully, has freely sent His Son, whose perfect obedience in the place of our sin and disobedience is given to us by grace alone, through faith alone. This is a story we must hear and learn over and over again. Because Christ's work is given to us, we are regarded by God "as if [we] had never committed nor had any sin," but even more, as if we "had [ourselves] accomplished all the obedience which Christ has rendered for [us]" (HC, Q&A 60). We are forgiven; we are righteous; we are "found in him" (Phil. 3:9). He calls to us now that we might call out to Him, "Lord, save me" (Matt. 14:30).

*Notes*

---

1   For several excellent books on the doctrine of justification, see Robert Trail, *Justification Vindicated*, Puritan Paperbacks (1692; repr., Edinburgh: Banner of Truth, 2002); James Buchanan, *The Doctrine of Justification: An Outline of its History in the Church and of its Exposition from Scripture* (1867; repr., Grand Rapids: Baker, 1955); R. C. Sproul, *Faith Alone: The Evangelical Doctrine of Justification* (Grand Rapids: Baker, 1995).

2   On the importance of understanding the difference between the law and the gospel, see John Colquhoun, *A Treatise of the Law and the Gospel* (1816; repr., Grand Rapids: Soli Deo Gloria, 2009).

3   From the hymn "Amazing Grace!" by John Newton, 1779. *Psalter Hymnal* (Grand Rapids: Christian Reformed Church, 1976), #380.

4   For an excellent book on the doctrine of Christ alone, see Sinclair B. Ferguson, *In Christ Alone: Living the Gospel-Centered Life* (Orlando, Fla.: Reformation Trust, 2007).

# Six

# SANCTIFICATION: THE CHRISTIAN LIFE

*We are not our own; therefore, neither is our own reason or will to rule our acts and counsels. We are not our own; therefore, let us not make it our end to seek what may be agreeable to our carnal nature. We are not our own; therefore, as far as possible, let us forget ourselves and the things that are ours. On the other hand, we are God's; let us, therefore, live and die to him (Rom. 14:8). We are God's; therefore, let his wisdom and will preside over all our actions. We are God's; to him, then, as the only legitimate end, let every part of our life be directed!*[1]

—John Calvin

God reconciles us to Himself and restores us to a relationship with Himself through the work of our Lord Jesus Christ. By His work, Jesus merited two great benefits for us. The first we saw in the last chapter—justification—and the second we will examine in this chapter—sanctification.[2] By justification, we are no longer under condemnation, as we are freed from the guilt of sin. However, the drama of God's work does not end there. It continues as God begins to work within us. By earning for us sanctification, Christ makes us new creatures. He begins to free us from the practical power of sin in our daily lives. In sanctification, God the Holy Spirit makes us more and more like Jesus, renewing us in the image of God (Rom. 8:29; Eph. 4:24; Col. 3:10).

Our Reformed fathers focused heavily on holy living. The volume of teachings they devoted to sanctification in their confessions and catechisms is striking. The Heidelberg Catechism devotes forty-four of its 129 questions and answers, more than one-third of its material, to sanctification, while the Westminster Larger Catechism devotes an impressive eighty-two of 196 questions and answers (42 percent) to this subject. By this emphasis, the Reformed churches declared that Calvinism is no mere religion of "head knowledge," and we cannot live as if it makes us the "frozen chosen," as we are sometimes derisively known. It is a religion of head *and* heart.

In their focus on sanctification, the Reformed churches sought to reorient the mind-set of Christians from thinking of godly living as legal to evangelical. This means that they saw obedience to God as not about guilt and legalism but as gospel-oriented.[3] We see this in the fact that the writers of the Heidelberg and Westminster Larger catechisms placed the Ten Commandments and Lord's Prayer at the end of their respective catechisms to show us that obedience is a response to the wonder of the gospel.

## NEW LIFE

In sanctifying us, Christ gives us a new life by the power of His Holy Spirit. As Paul said: "Therefore, if anyone is in Christ, he is a new creation. The old has passed away; behold, the new has come" (2 Cor. 5:17). The Belgic Confession speaks of the true faith that receives Jesus Christ alone for justification, saying it also "regenerates him and makes him a new man, causing him to live a new life, and freeing him from the bondage of sin" (BC, Art. 24). The confession uses the word *regenerates* in its older sense, that is, with reference to the entire new life we have in Christ.[4] This new life is the reason we do good works, according to the Heidelberg Catechism. After it asks, "Since, then, we are redeemed from our misery by grace through Christ, without any merit of ours, why must we do good works?" it answers, "Because Christ, having redeemed us by his blood, also renews us by his Holy Spirit after his own image" (HC, Q&A 86).

This new life is characterized by gratitude. The Heidelberg Catechism expresses this in its division into three parts, commonly known as guilt, grace, and gratitude. After its initial question on Christian comfort (HC, Q&A 1), the catechism asks, "How many things are necessary for thee to know, that thou in this comfort mayest live and die happily?" (Q&A 2). The answer is: "Three things: First, the greatness of my *sin* and *misery* [Q&A 3–11]. Second, how I am *redeemed* from all my sins and misery [Q&A 12–85]. Third, how I am to be *thankful* to God for such redemption [Q&A 86–129]."

In this third section on gratitude, the Heidelberg Catechism says that since we have been "redeemed from our misery by grace through Christ, without any merit of ours," our Lord Jesus Christ "renews us by His Holy Spirit after his own image, that with our whole life we show ourselves thankful to God for his blessing" (HC, Q&A 86).

Thus, the character of the Christian life is located in gratitude, not guilt. As noted above, that means it is evangelical, or gospel-oriented, not legal. This calling to obedience motivated by gratitude is movingly expressed in the Westminster Larger Catechism. Question 97 asks, "What special use is there of the moral law to the regenerate?" The answer states that although Christians are regenerated and delivered from the condemnation of the law, "it is of special use, to show them: How much they are bound to Christ for his fulfilling it, and enduring the curse thereof in their stead, and for their good; and thereby to provoke them to more thankfulness, and to express the same in their greater care to conform themselves thereunto as the rule of their obedience."

Sanctification teaches us that we are "bound" to Jesus Christ. Because of His obedience to the law and His death on our behalf, He causes us to be concerned with thankful obedience. Paul used the metaphor of a bondservant to express the contrast between our life before and after God made us new creatures:

What then? Are we to sin because we are not under law but under grace? By no means! Do you not know that if you present yourselves to anyone as obedient slaves, you are slaves of the one whom you obey, either of sin, which leads to death, or of obedience, which leads to righteousness? But thanks be to God, that you who were once slaves of sin have become obedient from the heart to the standard of teaching to which you were committed, and, having been set free from sin, have become slaves of righteousness. I am speaking in human terms, because of your natural limitations. For just as you once presented your members as slaves to impurity and to lawlessness leading to more lawlessness, so now present your members as slaves to righteousness leading to sanctification. For when you were slaves of sin, you were free in regard to righteousness. But what fruit were you getting at that time from the things of which you are now ashamed? For the end of those things is death. But now that you have been set free from sin and have become slaves of God, the fruit you get leads to sanctification and its end, eternal life. (Rom. 6:15–22)

## SCRIPTURAL ANALOGIES

What is the relationship between justification and sanctification, our being made right before God in Christ and our being made new practically? First, we must be clear that good works have no standing before God for our justification:

Therefore we do good works, but not to merit by them (for what can we merit?). . . . Moreover, though we do good works, we do not found our salvation upon them; for we can do no work but what is polluted by our flesh, and also punishable; and although we could perform such works, still the remembrance of one sin is sufficient to make God reject them. Thus, then, we would always be in doubt, tossed to and fro without any certainty, and our poor consciences would be continually vexed if they relied not on the merits of the suffering and death of our Savior. (BC, Art. 24; cf. HC, Q&A 62)

Instead, good works are the logical and necessary *result* of justification.

One of the ways the Reformed confessions describe this relationship is by using Jesus' analogy of a tree's roots and fruits. When our Lord spoke of false prophets, He said: "So, every healthy tree bears good fruit, but the diseased tree bears bad fruit. A healthy tree cannot bear bad fruit, nor can a diseased tree bear good fruit. Every tree that does not bear good fruit is cut down and thrown into the fire" (Matt. 7:17–19).

The Belgic Confession of Faith uses this vivid illustration to speak of good works when it says: "These works, as they proceed from the good root of faith, are good and acceptable in the sight of God, forasmuch as they are all sanctified by His grace. Nevertheless they are of no account towards our justification, for it is by faith in Christ that we are justified, even before we do good works; otherwise they could not be good works, any more than the fruit of a tree can be good before the tree itself is good" (BC, Art. 24).

This means that when we know that we are justified by faith alone apart from any and all works, we do not want to go on sinning. This was one of the objections Paul faced. When he preached grace so powerfully, saying, "Now the law came in to increase the trespass, but where sin increased, grace abounded all the more" (Rom. 5:20), people thought he was saying it does not matter how we live. He went on to ask: "What shall we say then? Are we to continue in sin that grace may abound? By no means! How can we who died to sin still live in it? Do you not know that all of us who have been baptized into Christ Jesus were baptized into his death? We were buried therefore with him by baptism into death, in order that, just as Christ was raised from the dead by the glory of the Father, we too might walk in newness of life" (Rom. 6:1–4).

The Heidelberg Catechism asks the question this way: "But does not this doctrine [justification by faith alone] make men careless and profane?" It answers with these words: "No, for it is impossible that those who are implanted into Christ by true faith, should not bring forth fruits of thankfulness" (HC, Q&A 64).

The Belgic Confession has a much more extensive treatment of this subject, saying:

> Therefore it is so far from being true that this justifying faith makes men remiss in a pious and holy life, that on the contrary without it they would never do anything out of love to God, but only out of self-love or fear of damnation. Therefore it is impossible that this holy faith can be unfruitful in man; for we do not speak of a vain faith, but of such a faith which is called in Scripture a faith working through love, which excites man to the practice of those works which God has commanded in His Word. (BC, Art. 24)

Sanctification is also described in Scripture as a death and resurrection. Again, Paul says, "We were buried therefore with him by baptism into death, in order that, just as Christ was raised from the dead by the glory of the Father, we too might walk in newness of life" (Rom. 6:4). Elsewhere, Paul applies this analogy to us practically and says believers are to "put to death therefore what is earthly in you . . . seeing that you have put off the old self with its practices and have put on the new self, which is being renewed in knowledge after the image of its creator" (Col. 3:5, 9–10). This dying and rising is what the Heidelberg Catechism calls "true repentance or conversion" (HC, Q&A 88). It then goes on to ask:

**What is the dying of the old man?**
Heartfelt sorrow for sin, causing us to hate and turn from it always more and more. (HC, Q&A 89)

**What is the making alive of the new man?**
Heartfelt joy in God through Christ, causing us to take delight in living according to the will of God in all good works. (HC, Q&A 90)

### THE LAW OF GOD

How do we know how to live "according to the will of God in all good works"? When we become new creatures in Christ, the Ten Commandments and the Lord's Prayer give structure to our life of gratitude. As Spirit-led people, we begin to perform those works that God has commanded in His law—the same that Adam rebelled against in the beginning and that we cannot perform before coming to Jesus Christ because of our fallen nature. The Word of God commands us to do good works according to the law of God. The law no longer condemns us or enslaves us; instead, it serves as a guide to lead us in a life of holiness before the Lord: "we still use the testimonies taken out of the law and the prophets to confirm us in the doctrine of the gospel, and to regulate our life in all honorableness to the glory of God, according to His will" (BC, Art. 25).

## Three Divisions

In classic Reformed theology, the law of God has a threefold division. First, there is the moral aspect of the law. This refers to everything in the law that expresses an abiding principle of who God is and who we are to be. This law is "summarily comprehended in the ten commandments" (WLC, Q&A 98). Second, there are the ceremonial aspects of the law, which are those things in Scripture that teach some religious truth leading people to the Messiah, Jesus Christ. For example, Paul speaks of the religious feast days of the old covenant, saying, "These are a shadow of the things to come, but the substance belongs to Christ" (Col. 2:17). Third, there is the judicial aspect, which refers to the punishments given in the law for those who transgressed the law.[5] John Calvin could call this way of viewing the law of God a "common division," and Philip Melanchthon (1497–1560) spoke of "The old and customary divisions."[6]

What does this threefold division mean? For example, in relation to the Sabbath commandment, the moral aspect was the cessation of labor in order to worship one day in seven (Ex. 20:8–11), the ceremonial aspect was doing this on the seventh day, and the judicial aspect was the death penalty for violations (Ex. 31:12–18). The moral aspect continues in all times and places, while the Westminster Confession of Faith says that the ceremonial laws "are now abrogated, under the new testament" (19.3), and the judicial laws "expired together with the state of that people [the ancient Israelites], not obliging any other now, further than the general equity thereof may require" (19.4).

## Three Uses

Classic Reformed theology also helps us understand that the law of God has three uses.[7] First, there is the pedagogical use (Latin, *usus pedagogicus*). This means that the law is a "tutor" to lead us to Christ by showing us our sins and our futile efforts to save ourselves (Gal. 3:24). Second, there is the civil use (Latin, *usus civilis*), which is the law used in society. This is the law that is written on the heart of man, by which, for example, all people know that murder is wrong, as well as the law that gives the general principles to restrain society from unbridled wickedness.[8] Third, there is the didactic use (Latin, *usus didacticus*). This is the law used as a guide for living as we respond in gratitude to Christ's amazing grace.

The Heidelberg Catechism elaborates on the role of the law in the Christian life:

### Can those who are converted to God keep these Commandments perfectly?

No, but even the holiest men, while in this life, have only a small beginning of such obedience, yet so that with earnest purpose they begin to live not only according to some, but according to all the Commandments of God. (HC, Q&A 114)

### Why then does God so strictly enjoin the Ten Commandments upon us, since in this life no one can keep them?

First, that as long as we live we may learn more and more to know our sinful nature, and so the more earnestly seek forgiveness of sins and righteousness in Christ; second, that without ceasing we diligently ask God for the grace of the Holy Spirit, that we be renewed more and more after the image of God, until we attain the goal of perfection after this life. (HC, Q&A 115)

How, then, does the law guide us in our life of sanctification? Briefly, here is what each of the Ten Commandments teaches:

• "Thou shalt have no other gods before me" (Ex. 20:3, KJV)—teaches us to love God by worshiping the one true God (HC, Q&A 94–95; WLC, Q&A 103–106).

• "Thou shalt not make unto thee any graven image" (Ex. 20:4, KJV)—teaches us to love God by worshiping Him according to His will (HC, Q&A 96–98; WLC, Q&A 107–110).

• "Thou shalt not take the name of the LORD thy God in vain" (Ex. 20:7, KJV)—teaches us to love God by speaking reverently of Him (HC, Q&A 99–102; WLC, Q&A 111–114).

• "Remember the sabbath day, to keep it holy" (Ex. 20:8, KJV)—teaches us to love God by worshiping Him when He commands (HC, Q&A 103; WLC, Q&A 115–121).

• "Honour thy father and thy mother" (Ex. 20:12, KJV)—teaches us to love our neighbor by honoring those in authority over us (HC, Q&A 104; WLC, Q&A 123–133).

• "Thou shalt not kill" (Ex. 20:13, KJV)—teaches us to love our neighbor by not murdering in thought, word, or deed (HC, Q&A 105–107; WLC, Q&A 134–136).

• "Thou shalt not commit adultery" (Ex. 20:14, KJV)—teaches us to love our neighbor by being pure (HC, Q&A 108–109; WLC, Q&A 137–139).

• "Thou shalt not steal" (Ex. 20:15, KJV)—teaches us to love our neighbor by providing for others' needs (HC, Q&A 110–111; WLC, Q&A 140–142).

• "Thou shalt not bear false witness against thy neighbour" (Ex. 20:16, KJV)—teaches us to love our neighbor by telling the truth (HC, Q&A 112; WLC, Q&A 143–145).

- "Thou shalt not covet" (Ex. 20:17, KJV)—teaches us to love our neighbor by being content with what God has given us (HC, Q&A 113; WLC, Q&A 146–148).[9]

### *Love*

As the above list of commands and their meanings shows, the law teaches us to love God and to love our neighbors. Why did I present it in that way? Because Jesus Christ Himself explained the law in this way:

> But when the Pharisees heard that he had silenced the Sadducees, they gathered together. And one of them, a lawyer, asked him a question to test him. "Teacher, which is the great commandment in the Law?" And he said to him, "You shall love the Lord your God with all your heart and with all your soul and with all your mind. This is the great and first commandment. And a second is like it: You shall love your neighbor as yourself. On these two commandments depend all the Law and the Prophets." (Matt. 22:34–40)

Of course, as we have already seen, while the law requires us to love God and neighbor, before Christ redeems us we are actually "lovers of self" (2 Tim. 3:2) and "lovers of pleasure rather than lovers of God" (2 Tim. 3:3). The wonderful truth is that when Christ redeems us and gives us His Holy Spirit, He changes our attitude and affections toward the law. Paul describes this by saying that we have been "released from the law, having died to that which held us captive, so that we serve in the new way of the Spirit and not in the old way of the written code" (Rom. 7:6). He adds, "I delight in the law of God, in my inner being" (Rom. 7:22).

So while the law does not change, we do. We are enabled by the power of the Holy Spirit to love God and neighbor, and the law is a guide that aids us in that. As Paul said, "Owe no one anything, except to love each other, for the one who loves another has fulfilled the law. . . . Love does no wrong to a neighbor; therefore love is the fulfilling of the law" (Rom. 13:8, 10). Now we are freed from the enslaving power of sin in order to serve: "For you were called to freedom, brothers. Only do not use your freedom as an opportunity for the flesh, but through love serve one another. For the whole law is fulfilled in one word: 'You shall love your neighbor as yourself'" (Gal. 5:13–14).

## THE LORD'S PRAYER

While the Ten Commandments give structure to how we live, the Lord's Prayer gives us structure as to how we pray and express our gratitude to God for our justification in Christ.

"Why is prayer necessary for Christians?" the Heidelberg Catechism asks. "Because it is the chief part of the thankfulness which God requires of us, and because God will give his grace and Holy Spirit only to such as earnestly and without ceasing beg them from him and render thanks unto him for them" (HC, Q&A 116).

While the Heidelberg asks "why," the Westminster Larger Catechism asks "what": "What is prayer?" It answers: "Prayer is an offering up of our desires unto God, in the name of Christ, by the help of his Spirit; with confession of our sins, and thankful acknowledgment of his mercies" (WLC, Q&A 178).

The Heidelberg Catechism describes the nature of true prayer in these words:

## What belongs to such prayer as God is pleased with and will hear?

First, that from the heart we call only upon the one true God, who has revealed himself to us in his Word, for all that he has commanded us to ask of him; secondly, that we thoroughly know our need and misery, so as to humble ourselves before the face of his divine majesty; thirdly, that we be firmly assured that, notwithstanding our unworthiness, he will, for the sake of Christ our Lord, certainly hear our prayer, as he has promised us in his Word. (HC, Q&A 117)

To guide us in prayer, God has given "the special rule of direction . . . that form of prayer which our Savior Christ taught his disciples, commonly called the Lord's Prayer" (WLC, Q&A 186). It is a pattern for prayer, as well as a prayer "done with understanding, faith, reverence, and other graces necessary to the right performance of the duty of prayer" (WLC, Q&A 187).

In this prayer, there is an invocation ("Our Father, who art in heaven"; HC, Q&A 120–121; WLC, Q&A 189), six petitions ("Hallowed be thy name"; "Thy kingdom come"; "Thy will be done in earth as it is in heaven"; "Give us this day our daily bread"; "Forgive us our debts, as we forgive our debtors"; and "And lead us not into temptation, but deliver us from evil"; HC, Q&A 122–127; WLC, Q&A 190–195), and a doxology ("For thine is the kingdom"; HC, Q&A 128–129; WLC, Q&A 196). The Larger Catechism explains the meaning of the invocation in a touching way, saying that our Lord teaches us in this prayer "to draw near to God with confidence of his fatherly goodness, and our interest therein; with reverence, and all other childlike dispositions, heavenly affections, and due

apprehensions of his sovereign power, majesty, and gracious conde-
scension: as also, to pray with and for others" (WLC, Q&A 189).

The Heidelberg Catechism closes with this short yet assuring
question and answer on the Lord's Prayer:

### What is the meaning of the word *Amen?*

*Amen* means: So shall it truly and surely be. For my prayer
is much more certainly heard of God than I feel in my heart
that I desire these things of him. (HC, Q&A 129)

## CONCLUSION

We have been justified once for all and we are being sanctified
throughout our lives by Jesus Christ through His powerful Holy
Spirit. Our lives are to be devoted to service. As Calvin said in the
opening quotation of this chapter, we belong to God. Martin Luther's
masterful summary of the Christian life still rings true today. At the
beginning of his profound treatise, *The Freedom of a Christian*, he
said: "To make the way smoother for the unlearned—for only them
do I serve—I shall set down the following two propositions concerning the freedom and the bondage of the spirit: a Christian is a
perfectly free lord of all, and subject to none; a Christian is a perfectly dutiful servant of all, subject to all."[10]

*Notes*

1  Calvin, *Institutes*, 3.7.1.

2  On sanctification, see Joel R. Beeke, *Living for God's Glory: An Introduction to
   Calvinism* (Orlando, Fla.: Reformation Trust, 2008); Walter Marshall, *The Gospel*

*Mystery of Sanctification* (Grand Rapids: Reformation Heritage Books, 1999); J. C. Ryle, *Holiness: Its Nature, Hindrances, Difficulties, and Roots* (1877; repr., Moscow, Ida.: Charles Nolan Publishers, 2001).

3  On gospel-driven sanctification, see Michael Horton, *The Gospel-Driven Life: Being Good News People in a Bad News World* (Grand Rapids: Baker, 2009).

4  For the narrower use of the term to describe the initial work of the Holy Spirit in making dead sinners alive, see the Canons of Dort, 3/4.10–13, 16.

5  For a brief and popular treatment in defense of the threefold division of the law, see Jonathan Bayes, *The Threefold Division of the Law* (Newcastle upon Tyne, England: The Christian Institute, 2005).

6  Calvin, *Institutes*, 4.20.14; Philip Melanchthon, *Melanchthon on Christian Doctrine: Loci Communes 1555*, trans. and ed. Clyde L. Manschreck (1965; repr., Grand Rapids: Baker, 1982), 83. For the roots of this threefold division in the medieval theologian Thomas Aquinas, see Stephen J. Casselli, "The Threefold Division of the Law in the Thought of Aquinas," *Westminster Theological Journal* 61:2 (Fall 1999): 175–207.

7  See Michael S. Horton, *The Law of Perfect Freedom* (Chicago: Moody Press, 1993), 31–33.

8  Sometimes the pedagogical and civil uses are reversed by various authors.

9  For several excellent expositions of the Ten Commandments, see the following: J. Douma, *The Ten Commandments: Manual for the Christian Life*, trans. Nelson D. Kloosterman (Phillipsburg, N.J.: P&R, 1996). This volume seeks to exposit the commandments biblically, historically, and theologically, and offers excellent material on how the commandments apply to modern ethical issues. Also, J. V. Fesko, *The Rule of Love: Broken, Fulfilled, and Applied* (Grand Rapids: Reformation Heritage Books, 2009). This book is a basic exposition with study questions. Also, Herman Witsius, *Sacred Dissertations on The Lord's Prayer*, trans. William Pringle (1839; repr., Phillipsburg, N.J.: P&R, 1994). This is a classic Dutch Puritan exposition.

10 Martin Luther, *Three Treatises* (second revised ed., Minneapolis: Fortress Press, 1970), 277.

# Seven

# CHURCH: DISTINGUISHING MARKS

*Well then, the Children's Creed teaches us (as was said) that a Christian holy people is to be and to remain on earth until the end of the world. . . . But how will or how can a poor confused person tell where such Christian holy people are to be found in this world?*[1]

—Martin Luther, 1539

One memorable event of my childhood was a time when my "grandpa" took only me out to lunch at a local smorgasbord. Since I did not know what a smorgasbord was or what I was supposed to do, he explained to me that there would be a large table with all kinds of food. Then he told me what I thought was the best part: "You get to pick and choose anything you would like."

Sadly, we live in an age in which the church is viewed more or less as a smorgasbord. There are all kinds and types of churches, providing consumers multiple options from which to pick and choose what they like.[2] This was somewhat true in the time of the Reformation, as there were Roman Catholic, Orthodox, Anabaptist, Lutheran, and Reformed churches. Today the situation is even more confusing, since so many organizations call themselves churches. We have everything from theological cults, such as the Church of Jesus Christ of Latter-day Saints, to thousands of garden-variety nondenominational churches, to the so-called "mainline" churches, and everything in between. The Belgic Confession's words are just as true today as they were when originally penned: "all sects which are in the world assume to themselves the name of the Church" (Art. 29).

As we saw in chapter three, the Protestant Reformers declared that the Word of God gave birth to the church, not vice versa, as the Roman Catholic Church taught. It is the preaching of the gospel of Jesus Christ, then, that creates the people of God. The gospel not only saves us from our sins and the wrath of God, it places us in vital union with Jesus Christ and other Christians. Thus, the church is the fruit of the gospel; it is not our own creation, but a creation of the triune God of grace. As the famous hymn says:

> The Church's one foundation is Jesus Christ her Lord,
> She is His new creation by water and the Word.
> From heaven He came and sought her to be His holy bride;
> With His own blood He bought her and for her life He died.[3]

The question is, how can we cut through all the claims of so many churches and identify the true churches? In this chapter, I want to examine the outward marks that the Reformed churches have long regarded as essential to the existence of a true church of God, marks that any Christian may use to judge the soundness of a church.

## WHICH CHURCH?

The Reformers searched the Word of God to answer the question of which churches were actually churches. Although there was some debate between Lutheran and Reformed theologians, and even among Reformed theologians themselves, the Reformed churches eventually settled on the belief that the Word revealed three essential outward marks by which any discerning person could determine whether any given congregation was truly a church: "The marks by which the true Church is known are these: If the pure doctrine of the gospel is preached therein; if it maintains the pure administration of the sacraments as instituted by Christ; if church discipline is exercised in punishing sin" (BC, Art. 29).[4]

These three marks of a true church—pure preaching of the gospel, pure administration of the sacraments, and church discipline—are in contrast with the marks of a false church, as the Belgic Confession continues: "As for the false Church, it ascribes more power and authority to itself and its ordinances than to the Word of God, and will not submit itself to the yoke of Christ. Neither does it administer the sacraments as appointed by Christ in His Word, but adds to and takes from, as it thinks proper; it relies more upon men than upon Christ; and persecutes those who live holily according to the Word of God and rebuke it for its errors, covetousness, and idolatry" (BC, Art. 29).

The Reformed churches are not motivated to talk about "true" churches and "false" churches by ego or arrogance, but by a sincere desire to see all God's sons and daughters in churches that feed their souls. We certainly pray that the Holy Spirit will grant us continued resolve to purely preach the gospel, purely administer the sacraments, and exercise church discipline, and that He would protect us from ascribing more power and authority to ourselves than to the Word, from refusing to submit ourselves to the yoke of Christ, from adding to and taking from Christ's sacraments, from relying more on men than on Christ, and from persecuting those who live godly lives. We pray these things will be true of us because of God's purpose for His church: "Unto this catholic visible Church Christ hath given the ministry, oracles, and ordinances of God, for the gathering and perfecting of the saints, in this life, to the end of the world: and doth by his own presence and Spirit, according to his promise, make them effectual thereunto" (WCF, 25.3).

## THE PURE PREACHING OF THE GOSPEL

The most fundamental of the three marks is the pure preaching of the gospel. Apart from the gospel preached, there is no church.

We see this in the example of our Lord, who began His earthly ministry by preaching—"From that time Jesus began to preach, saying, 'Repent, for the kingdom of heaven is at hand'" (Matt. 4:17)—and concluded it by sending out His apostles to preach and continue His work—"Go therefore and make disciples of all nations . . . teaching them to observe all that I have commanded you. And behold, I am with you always, to the end of the age" (Matt. 28:19–20).

The apostle Paul addressed the importance of preaching the doctrine of justification when he said:

How then will they call on him in whom they have not believed? And how are they to believe in him of whom they have never heard? And how are they to hear without someone preaching?

And how are they to preach unless they are sent? As it is written, "How beautiful are the feet of those who preach the good news." But they have not all obeyed the gospel. For Isaiah says, "Lord, who has believed what he has heard from us?" So faith comes from hearing, and hearing through the word of Christ. (Rom. 10:14–17)

To purely preach the gospel, a minister must preach the doctrine I described in chapter five—that sinners are justified by the free grace of God alone, which is received through faith alone, which itself is a gift of God, and that this faith is placed in and rests on nothing except Jesus Christ the Righteous. Churches must see to it, in the words of the famous hymn, that those in the pew understand, "My hope is built on nothing less, than Jesus' blood and righteousness."[5] It was the loss of this truth in the Roman Catholic Church that so troubled the Reformers. As the Italian Reformer Peter Martyr Vermigli (1499–1562) said about the Catholic Church, "They have undoubtedly corrupted doctrine, since they deny what Scripture affirms: that we are justified by faith alone."[6]

The Reformers understood justification to be purely preached when the Word is "rightly handl[ed]" (2 Tim. 2:15). A part of using the Word properly involves recognizing that it has two elements: law and gospel. The law is to be preached in all its terror, while the gospel is to be preached in all its comfort as that which the law cannot do (Rom. 8:3–4; CD, 3/4.6). Simply put, the Reformers taught us to preach Christ crucified (1 Cor. 1:23). If a church preaches any other "gospel," whether it is explicitly faith plus works or some insidious version of "get in by faith, stay in by obedience," it is not in conformity with the "teaching of Christ" (2 John 9) but with that of

an antichrist counterfeit. Anything other than the doctrine of justification *sola fide* is what Paul termed "a different gospel" (Gal. 1:6),
which brings with it an eternal anathema (Gal. 1:8–9).

## THE PURE ADMINISTRATION
## OF THE SACRAMENTS

The second mark of a true church is the pure administration of the
sacraments. The two sacraments that Christ Himself instituted are
baptism (Matt. 28:18–20) and the Lord's Supper (Matt. 26:26–29).
Because of our continuing struggle with sin, the visible Word of the
sacraments supplements the audible Word of the gospel preached,
for God "hath joined [the sacraments] to the word of the gospel, the
better to present to our senses, both that which he signifies to us
by his Word, and that which he works inwardly in our hearts" (BC,
Art. 33). As the preaching of the gospel creates faith, the sacraments
confirm that faith within us (HC, Q&A 65), just as circumcision did
for Abraham, being "a seal (confirmation) of the righteousness that
he had by faith" (Rom. 4:11).

To purely administer the sacraments, a church must do so "as
instituted by Christ" (BC, Art. 29). This means, first, that it recog-
nizes that there are only the two sacraments—baptism and the Lord's
Supper—and that it therefore rejects the five other sacraments of the
Roman Catholic Church as false sacraments (HC, Q&A 68). Second,
this means that it administers the sacraments without the unbiblical ceremonies and elements that have been added to them over the
course of history, such as we find in the Roman Catholic Church.

Baptism is to be administered simply with water, in the name
of the triune God, and by an ordained minister (Matt. 28:18–20).

Whether one is baptized in a church building or at the beach; whether the baptism is done from a font or in a pool; whether it is performed by sprinkling, pouring, or immersion; and whether the minister sprinkles, pours, or immerses once or three times is all indifferent.[7] The Lord's Supper is purely administered when bread (whether leavened or unleavened) and wine are given to those who profess faith and are members of Christ's church, whether kneeling, sitting, or standing.[8] This is to be done with the recitation of the words of institution (as the example of Paul testifies in 1 Cor. 11:23–26), the breaking of the bread (" . . . he took bread . . . he broke it . . . "), and prayer over the bread and wine (" . . . when he had given thanks . . . ").[9]

## THE EXERCISE OF CHURCH DISCIPLINE

The third mark of a true church, church discipline, has a largely negative connotation in our culture, but the biblical idea is both positive and negative.

A person is brought into the church by baptism and is nourished, or disciplined, by the preaching of the gospel and the administration of the Lord's Supper. All true believers need to be disciplined by these means until the Lord comes again; therefore, they should receive the preaching of the Word from their pastors and partake of the Lord's Supper when it is served by the church elders. By these means, church leaders carry out the positive form of church discipline. It is positive in the sense that members are encouraged, built up, and strengthened through God's appointed means and appointed messengers. Scripture exhorts believers to "obey your leaders and submit to them, for they are keeping watch over your souls, as those who will have to give an account. Let them do this with joy and not with groaning, for that would be of no advantage to you" (Heb. 13:17). By contrast, discipline in its negative form involves the "punishing of sin" (BC, Art. 29) in those who are unrepentant.

Discipline promotes God's holiness (Ezek. 36:16–21; 1 Cor. 5:1–5), protects the church from infection (1 Cor. 5:6; Heb. 12:15–16; 2 Tim. 2:14, 16–18), and restores the rebellious, making clear the seriousness of their resistance to Christ's Word and church (1 Cor. 5:5; 2 Cor. 2:5–11; Heb. 3:12–13; 10:24–25; 12:11–16).

## CONCLUSION

Where can seekers of the truth find the authentic Jesus Christ, His authentic gospel, an authentic church? By looking for the three biblical marks of preaching, the administration of the two sacraments, and the exercise of godly church discipline, the diligent and discriminating person may find the genuine article. With so many "churches" in any given local community, it is imperative that one find a congregation that is a true Christian "church," one in which Jesus Christ truly meets with His people in Word and sacrament, and shepherds them by the discipline of His undershepherds, the pastors and elders.

*Notes*

1   Martin Luther, "On the Councils and the Church," in Martin Luther's Basic Theological Writings, ed. Timothy F. Lull (Minneapolis: Fortress Press, 1989), 545.

2   On this modern deformation of the church into a consumer item, see Michael S. Horton, "Seekers or Tourists? Or the Difference Between Pilgrimage and Vacation," *Modern Reformation* 10:4 (July/August 2001): 12–18.

3   From the hymn "The Church's One Foundation" by Samuel J. Stone, 1866.

4   For some of this historical debate, see Daniel R. Hyde, *With Heart and Mouth: An*

*Exposition of the Belgic Confession* (Grandville, Mich.: Reformed Fellowship, 2008).

5 From the hymn "My Hope Is Built on Nothing Less" by Edward Mote, 1834.

6 Peter Martyr Vermigli, "Whether Evangelicals Are Schismatics for Having Separated from the Papists," in *Early Writings*, The Peter Martyr Library, Vol. One, trans. Mariano Di Gangi and Joseph C. McLelland, ed. Joseph C. McLelland (Kirksville, Mo.: Truman State University Press, 1994), 175.

7 On the mode of baptism, see Daniel R. Hyde, *Jesus Loves the Little Children: Why We Baptize Children* (Grandville, Mich.: Reformed Fellowship, 2006), 55–63.

8 There was debate over the posture of kneeling at the Lord's Supper. Among the English Reformers, this was an issue because of its association with the Roman Catholic Church's belief that believers adored the bread because it was literally and physically the body of Christ. In the 1552 *Book of Common Prayer*, the so-called "Black Rubric" (because it was printed in black ink in later editions) was added at the end of the Holy Communion service; it said in part of kneeling: "Which thing being well meant for a signification of the humble and grateful acknowledging of the benefits of Christ, given unto the worthy receiver, and to avoid the profanation and disorder, which about the holy Communion might else ensue: Lest yet the same kneeling might be thought or taken otherwise, we do declare that it is not meant thereby, that any adoration is done, or ought to be done, either unto the Sacramental bread or wine there bodily received, or unto any real and essential presence there being of Christ's natural flesh and blood. For as concerning the Sacramental bread and wine, they remain still in their very natural substances, and therefore may not be adored, for that were Idolatry to be abhorred of all faithful Christians. And as concerning the natural body and blood of our savior Christ, they are in heaven and not here. For it is against the truth of Christ's true natural body, to be in more places than in one, at one time." On this issue, see Peter Toon, *Which Rite is Right? The Eucharistic Prayer in the Anglican Tradition* (Swedesboro, N.J.: Preservation Press, 1994), 41–54; Samuel Leuenberger, *Archbishop Cranmer's Immortal Bequest: The Book of Common Prayer of the Church of England, An Evangelistic Liturgy*, trans. Samuel Leuenberger and Lewis J. Gorin, Jr. (1990; repr., Eugene, Ore.: Wipf & Stock, 2004), 123.

9 For a historical discussion of the Reformed insistence on the necessity of breaking the bread in communion versus the Lutheran doctrine and practice, see Bodo Nischan, "The 'Fracio Panis': A Reformed Communion Practice in Late Reformation Germany," *Church History* 53 (1984): 17–29; Daniel R. Hyde, "Lutheran Puritanism? *Adiaphora* in Lutheran Orthodoxy and Possible Commonalities in Reformed Orthodoxy," *American Theological Inquiry* 2:1 (January 2009): 61–83.

# Eight

# WORSHIP:
# OF GOD, BY GOD, FOR GOD

> *Worship is the submission of all of our nature to God.*
> *It is the quickening of conscience by His holiness,*
> *nourishment of mind by His truth, purifying of*
> *imagination by His beauty, opening of the heart to*
> *His love, and submission of will to His purpose, and*
> *all this gathered up in adoration is the greatest of*
> *human expressions of which we are capable.*[1]
>
> —William Temple, archbishop of Canterbury (1881–1944)

Why do we exist? This is one of the greatest philosophical and theological questions man has been attempting to answer for millennia. As Christians, we ask the question within the context of our covenant relationship with God: for what purpose did an all-sufficient God, who needs nothing besides Himself, decide to create us? The Westminster Larger Catechism asks the question this way: "What is the chief and highest end of man?" It answers: "Man's chief and highest end is to glorify God, and fully to enjoy him forever" (Q&A 1; cf.

WSC, Q&A 1). In short, we exist not only to give God glory, as we speak to God in worship through prayer and praise, but also to enjoy Him as He speaks to us in worship through Word and sacrament.

Because Scripture is our ultimate authority, it defines not only our theology but our piety, what we believe about God and how we respond to Him. Piety, then, is our grateful response to what God has done. John Calvin described piety as "that reverence joined with love of God which the knowledge of his benefits induces."[2] The psalmist spoke this way when he said, "Worship the LORD with reverence, and rejoice with trembling" (Ps. 2:11, NASB). The chief and highest way this reverential love is expressed is in public worship, which is the subject of this chapter.

One aspect that distinguished the Reformed churches from their co-Protestant Lutheran churches was their zeal to engage in the worship of God only on the basis of what the Word of God commanded or implicitly required. To adapt Abraham Lincoln's "Gettysburg Address," the Reformers believed that worship is of God, by God, and for God. For the Reformed, this meant that all unbiblical ceremonies were abolished for public worship. In fact, Calvin was so adamant about this point that he said the entire project of the Protestant Reformation was about worshiping God in a way that was pleasing to Him.[3] This point even led the great English matriarch, Queen Elizabeth I (1533–1603), to describe the Reformed churches on the continent of Europe as "more reformed" than the Lutheran churches.[4]

## THE WORD AND WORSHIP

The Belgic Confession of Faith links the Reformed churches' belief in the sufficiency of the Word of God to the area of worship when it says, "For since the whole manner of worship which God requires of us is written in them at large, it is unlawful for any one, though an Apostle, to teach otherwise than we are now taught in the Holy Scriptures: *nay, though it were an angel from heaven*, as the Apostle Paul saith" (Art. 7). "The whole manner of worship which God requires" is found in the Scriptures. This means we come to worship on God's terms, not ours; that we do in worship what God wants, not what we want.[5]

Continuing in a later section, the Belgic Confession says: ". . . we reject all human inventions, and all laws which man would introduce into the worship of God, thereby to bind and compel the conscience in any manner whatever. Therefore we admit only of that which tends to nourish and preserve concord and unity, and to keep all men in obedience to God" (Art. 32).

The Word, then, contains all we need in order to know how to worship; therefore, we reject all human-made laws or elements of worship. This is most memorably and succinctly stated in the Heidelberg Catechism, which says:

**What does God require in the second commandment?**
That we in no wise make any image of God, nor worship him in any other way than he has commanded us in his Word. (Q&A 96)

Over the centuries, Reformed churches came to call these ideas the "Regulative Principle of Worship."[6] The Regulative Principle of Worship holds that we worship God in the manner He has commanded us in His Word. As the Westminster Confession says, "But the acceptable way of worshipping the true God is instituted by himself, and so limited to his own revealed will, that he may not be worshipped according to the imaginations and devices of men, or the suggestions of Satan, under any visible representations or any other way not prescribed in the Holy Scripture" (21.1).

In the Reformed churches, we hold to this principle because we take the Bible seriously. It is God's Word to us for our faith, as well as for our worship and Christian life. Scripture alone is our ultimate rule, and it sufficiently gives us "all things that pertain to life and godliness" (2 Peter 1:3). So it alone governs the substance of what we do in worship.[7]

## OLD TESTAMENT

We see this principle taught in the Old Testament. God is jealous for His name to be revered and hallowed (Ex. 20:7; 34:13–14; Deut. 4:24; cf. Matt. 6:9). When we are jealous for His glory by worshiping Him as He deserves and desires, we "serve God acceptably with reverence and godly fear" (Heb. 12:28, KJV).

### *The Second Commandment*
In the first commandment, the one true God commands us to worship Him alone: "Thou shalt have no other gods before me" (Ex. 20:3, KJV). In the second commandment, this one true God tells us how we are *not* to worship Him: "Thou shalt not make unto thee any graven image" (Ex. 20:4, KJV; cf. Deut. 4:15–19). The second commandment also states that the "steadfast love" of God is toward those who "love me and keep my commandments" (Ex. 20:6). Intricately linked with the prohibition of images of God is the language of doing what the Lord says in His Word. The book of Leviticus also mentions

116

repeatedly that worship is "according to the rule" (e.g., Lev. 9:16; cf. Lev. 10:1; Deut. 12:29–32). Thus, all worship not "according to Scripture" is what Paul calls "will-worship" (Col. 2:23, ASV), a term the Reformers and the Puritans adopted. For example. Calvin said this word meant "a voluntary worship which men chose of their own will, without a command from God."[8] The English Puritan Richard Sibbes (1577–1636) stated it more simply and starkly when he called will-worship "a device of their own brain, a brat, a child of their own begetting."[9]

At the end of the Ten Commandments, this matter is stated in an unforgettable way: "If you make me an altar of stone, you shall not build it of hewn stones, for if you wield your tool on it you profane it" (Ex. 20:25). If the ancient Israelites were to think they could improve on the worship commanded of God by carving a more beautiful altar, they needed to know that even one mark added by the hand of man to what God had commanded was a complete contamination as far as God was concerned. When men try to improve the worship of God, they ruin that worship rather than improve it.

This commandment is impressed on the people of God with the injunction that the Lord is a "jealous" God. This is the language of marriage. The Lord has forsaken all others for His bride, Israel, and He loves and desires Her only.[10] When it comes to worship, then, He expects and desires Israel to respond with the same zeal for Him that He has for her.

### Cain and Abel

Adam and Eve had two sons, Cain and Abel. Cain was a farmer, a "worker of the ground," while his brother Abel, also a farmer, specialized in livestock as "a keeper of sheep" (Gen. 4:2). Cain offered God an offering "of the fruit of the ground"; Abel offered "the firstborn of his flock and of their fat portions" (vv. 3–4). God accepted Abel's offering but did not accept Cain's (vv. 4–5). Why?

They both offered an offering of worship. They both seemed "sincere"—the one principle, according to many today, that must guide worship. Yet God accepted Abel's offering and not Cain's because Abel offered what God commanded, that is, the best of what he had. The best, and the best alone, is fitting for worship. On the contrary, Cain offered what *he* thought worked or what *he* thought was best. Abel offered "the firstborn" of his flock and their "fat portions." These terms are used later in the law when God speaks of offering "the best of the firstfruits of your ground" (Ex. 34:26), as well as the firstborn of animals (Ex. 34:19; Lev. 27:26).[11]

Yet we must keep in mind that performing the correct rite is meaningless apart from faith. As Hebrews 11:4 teaches us, Abel offered a more acceptable sacrifice than Cain by faith, and through his sacrifice God testified to him that he was righteous. By faith Abel understood that just as the Lord God spared Adam and Eve by sacrificing animals in their place and covering them with the skins (Gen. 3:21), he could be acceptable to God only through the offering of another that would take his place and make satisfaction for his sins.[12]

### Nadab and Abihu

In the familiar yet fearful story of Nadab and Abihu, the brothers offered up "unauthorized fire before the LORD" (Lev. 10:1). In the preceding verses, we read that their father, Aaron, had offered the first sacrifices in the liturgical life of Israel. In Aaron's case, "fire came out from before the LORD and consumed the burnt offering . . . " (Lev. 9:24), yet in Nadab and Abihu's case, "fire came out from before the LORD and consumed *them*" (Lev. 10:2, emphasis added). Both Aaron and his sons were priests and offered sacrifices, yet the reason for God's differing responses was that Aaron offered a sacrifice "as the LORD commanded . . . according to the rule" (Lev. 9:10, 16), while Nadab and Abihu "offered unauthorized fire," that is, worship that was not commanded and therefore forbidden. Calvin said of this text:

> Apparently it was a light transgression to use strange fire for burning incense; and again their thoughtlessness would seem excusable, for certainly Nadab and Abihu did not wantonly or intentionally desire to pollute the sacred things, but, as is often the case in matters of novelty, when they were setting about them too eagerly, their precipitancy led them into error. The severity of the punishment, therefore, would not please those arrogant people, who do not hesitate superciliously to criticise God's judgments; but if we reflect how holy a thing God's worship is, the enormity of the punishment will by no means offend us. . . . Their crime is specified, viz., that they offered incense in a different way from that which God had prescribed, and consequently, although they may have erred from ignorance, still they were convicted by God's commandment of having negligently set about what was worthy of greater attention.[13]

The story of Nadab and Abihu is about worshiping God according to His Word, not according to one's own desire, however sincere.

To offer worship not prescribed was to profane God and take away from His glory. This is why, after Nadab and Abihu were consumed, God, through Moses, said to Aaron, "Among those who are near me I will be sanctified, and before all the people I will be glorified" (Lev. 10:3). Calvin applied this text to his hearers in this way: "Let us learn, therefore, so to attend to God's command as not to corrupt His worship by any strange inventions."[14]

Because of His holiness and glory, God prescribed not only that the Israelites were to worship Him, but how they were to do so. Thus, the place of worship, the tabernacle, was to be made "according to the pattern that was shown you" (Heb. 8:5; cf. Ex. 25:9, 40; 26:30; 27:8; Num. 8:4; Acts 7:44), just as the acts of worship, the sacrifices, were to be offered "according to the rule."

## NEW TESTAMENT

You might be thinking, "But this is all Old Testament teaching." Yet Jesus said, "Go therefore and make disciples of all nations, baptizing them . . . teaching them to observe all that I have commanded you" (Matt. 28:19–20). Is the solemn requirement that the church teach all things that Christ has commanded not also a solemn prohibition against teaching anything that He has *not* commanded? If, in the worship of God, we observe all that Christ has commanded, ought we not also scrupulously avoid anything and everything that He has not commanded?

Jesus said that the Pharisees worshiped God "in vain" (Mark 7:7). Why did God reject their worship? Because, Jesus said, "You leave the commandment of God," preferring "the tradition of men" (Mark 7:7–8). They worshiped God in vain because they worshiped

God as they wished, not as God required. In the same way, the apostle Paul warned the Colossians, "Let no one disqualify you, insisting on asceticism and worship of angels, going on in detail about visions, puffed up without reason by his sensuous mind" (Col. 2:18). Paul was speaking here of the worship people wished to offer in the way *they* wished to offer it, rather than worship as God commanded it: "These have indeed an appearance of wisdom in promoting self-made religion and asceticism and severity to the body, but they are of no value in stopping the indulgence of the flesh" (Col. 2:23). This "self-made religion" was the equivalent of "will-worship," which is literally what the Greek word stands for.[15]

No doubt Jesus was rude by our standards when He said to the Samaritan woman at the well, "You worship what you do not know; we worship what we know, for salvation is from the Jews" (John 4:22). But He was only being truthful. "God is spirit," He said, "and those who worship him must worship in spirit and truth" (John 4:24). True worship was impossible for the Samaritans as long as they worshiped God as they wished. They needed to worship God as He commanded in order to find acceptance with Him. "True worshipers . . . worship the Father in spirit and truth," Jesus said, and "the Father is seeking such people to worship him" (John 4:23). When we persist in worshiping God as we will, rather than as God wills, we are not "true worshipers."

In Romans 1:21–25, the apostle Paul condemns every kind of false worship invented by men. He also reveals the source of such false worship. Men become "vain in their imaginations," he says (v. 21, KJV). They invent what they vainly imagine to be good ways to worship. They worship as they want, not as God commands. But when they do this, they really "worship and serve the creature rather than the Creator," says Paul (v. 25), and for this reason "they are without excuse" (v. 20). They are without excuse because there is no excuse for departing from the rule that we must not worship God "in any other way than he has commanded us in his Word."

## THE DAY OF WORSHIP

As we saw earlier, the first four commandments of the law teach us how to love God, even how to love Him in worship on the day of His choosing.[16] It is important for us to understand the fourth commandment, in which God gives His command for the day of His worship: "Remember the Sabbath day, to keep it holy" (Ex. 20:8). How are we as Christians to observe this commandment?

### From Sabbath to Sunday

From creation onward, the people of God worshiped on the seventh day of the week. This was a "creation ordinance" that the Creator Himself established by His example, with the intent that His creatures would follow it. He worked six days and called His image-bearers to work (Gen. 2:15); He rested on the seventh day (Gen. 2:2; Ex. 20:11; 31:17) and called His image-bearers to rest. He signified this with His benediction, setting apart the seventh day as "holy" (Gen. 2:3).

Later, when the Sabbath command was reiterated, we read: "In six days the LORD made heaven and earth, and on the seventh day he rested and was refreshed" (Ex. 31:17). The word *refreshed* (Hebrew, *naphash*) is used only two other times in the Old Testament: once in reference to giving rest to animals, servants, and visitors within Israel (Ex. 23:12), and once in reference to David and his men (2 Sam. 16:14). After God worked to make everything, it was as if His rest refreshed Him. Yet God's rest and refreshment mean so much more; they have to do with His joy and satisfaction. The psalmist writes, "May the LORD rejoice in his works" (Ps. 104:31). God's rest and satisfaction was that of a King; having created the heavens and the earth to be His cosmic palace, He took His place on His throne, so to speak, on the seventh day.

After God brought His people out of Egypt and through the Red Sea, the Sabbath day took on even more significance as a covenant sign that God sanctified His people (Ex. 31:13). On that day, the saints celebrated the reality that God had created them and that their rest was rooted in His rest: "For in six days the LORD made heaven and earth, the sea, and all that is in them, and rested the seventh day" (Ex. 20:8–11). As well, the Sabbath signified that God had redeemed His people (Deut. 5:12–15). Finally, the annual Day of Atonement fell on a Sabbath (Lev. 16:30–31), so the Sabbath also celebrated God's forgiveness of His people.

Under the old covenant with Israel (Ex. 19; Heb. 8:6, 7, 13), the Sabbath day was extremely strict. Not only was no work to be done by the Israelites and their children, they also were to give rest to all in their households—servants, livestock, even sojourners (Ex. 20:10). God even gave regulatory laws over what could and could not be done. For example, if one even went out to gather sticks on the Sabbath in order to kindle a fire (Num. 15:32–36; Ex. 35:1–3), he was to be put to death (Ex. 31:14–15; 35:2). All this strictness was a part of the tutelage of the law, which was meant to lead Israel by the hand to Jesus Christ (Gal. 3:24), who is the final sacrifice ending the old covenant (Heb. 7:11–12, 18–19; 8:7, 13).

When Jesus rose from the dead on the first day of the week,

things changed. Christ, the second Adam, "finished" (John 19:30) the work that the first Adam failed to do (Rom. 5:12–19). Because of that pivotal event, the church determined that for Christians under the new covenant, the day of worship and celebration of the Lord's grace in Jesus Christ was to be the first day of the week, Sunday: "From the beginning of the world to the resurrection of Christ, [the Sabbath] was the last day of the week; and, from the resurrection of Christ, was changed into the first day of the week, which, in Scripture, is called the Lord's day, and is to be continued to the end of the world, as the Christian Sabbath" (WCF, 21:7). On this day, we are reminded of and participate in the glorious reality that we have already entered God's rest (Matt. 11:28; Heb. 4:10) and that we await the experience of the fullness of this rest in eternity in the new heavens and new earth (Rev. 21–22). We now assemble corporately for worship and enjoy a foretaste of our eternal rest, then go out into the kingdom of this world to work for six days.

So why do we worship on Sunday and not Saturday?

• The first day of the week was the day on which our Lord rose from the dead (John 20:1; cf. Ps. 118:24).

• The first day of the week is called "the Lord's day" (Rev. 1:10; cf. 1 Cor. 16:2).

• The first day was the day on which the Holy Spirit was poured out on the church (Acts 2:1–36).

• Just as on the first day of creation God made light and separated it from the darkness, we gather on the first day of the week to celebrate the light of the gospel in Jesus Christ, who has separated us from the world of the darkness of sin (John 1:5, 9; 3:19; 8:12; 2 Cor. 4:1–6).

### *From Creation to Re-Creation*

From creation until Christ, the people of God worked six days and then rested on the seventh day. This was a picture of their looking forward to eternal rest; the seventh day of creation was not structured with an "evening and morning" as the previous six days (Gen. 2:1–3), which signified that the seventh day had no end and was thus a foretaste of eternity itself. On the other hand, from the work of Christ until the consummation, the people of God rest on the first day and work the next six, looking back on the finished work of Christ. Yet we too look forward to the full consummation of this rest.

When our Lord lay in the tomb from Friday evening through early Sunday morning, the old order of things was buried with Him; when He rose again, He began a new order of things. This is why the Gospel of John speaks of the first day of the week as the eighth day, literally, "after eight days" (20:26). It was not just the beginning of another week, but, in fact, a new beginning. This was because the resurrection of Christ was the firstfruits of the final resurrection and restoration of all things (Rom. 8:18–25; 1 Cor. 15:23). On the Lord's Day, our worship is a commemoration of Christ's accomplished work and triumphant resurrection, and an anticipation of the day of re-creation, when the Lord shall make all things new (Rev. 21:4–5). But it is also a participation in the age to come already in this age. As Paul says, upon us "the end of the ages has come" (1 Cor. 10:11). We have entered this Sabbath rest, according to the writer to the Hebrews: "For we who have believed enter that rest . . . for whoever has entered God's rest has also rested from his works as God did from his" (Heb. 4:3, 10).

### Letting the Lord's Day Structure Us

All of this teaches us that instead of seeing the Lord's Day as a rule that stifles our "weekend," we need to view it as a gift from God that actually structures our lives. The practice of the Lord's Day is not legalism, but it is a part of our piety, providing us physical and spiritual rest. We sanctify the day because we belong not to this age that is passing away but to the glorious age to come. We need to acknowledge, then, that Sunday is the Lord's *Day* and not the Lord's *morning* (or, sadly, the Lord's *hour*), just as the Sabbath was a *day* of rest.

As Christians, we have been liberated from "the land of Egypt, . . . [from] the house of slavery" (Ex. 20:2; Deut. 5:6), which is the enslaving power of sin and Satan. Now we are "slaves of God" (Rom. 6:22). As His servants, we are to give ourselves to self-sacrificial worship of God, through Christ, in the power of the Spirit (Rom. 12:1–2; Eph. 2:18). We are to set aside the Lord's Day to remember our creation (Ex. 20:11) and re-creation (Deut. 5:15) in public worship. This is what the Heidelberg Catechism says when it answers the question, "What does God require in the fourth commandment?" Notice that the answer does not contain a laundry list of "do's" and "don'ts," but simply says,

> In the first place, that the ministry of the Gospel and schools be maintained; and that I, especially on the day of rest, diligently attend church, to learn the Word of God, to use the holy Sacraments, to call publicly upon the Lord, and to give Christian alms. (Q&A 103)

Since Sunday is *the Lord's* Day, it is His will for us that we diligently attend church, "not neglecting to meet together, as is the habit of some, but encouraging one another, and all the more as you see the Day drawing near" (Heb. 10:25). This diligence in anticipation of the final day is seen in the early Christians, who "devoted themselves to the apostles' teaching and fellowship, to the breaking of bread and the prayers" (Acts 2:42). Setting aside Sunday means that we are to commit ourselves to gratefully resting and worshiping the triune God because we belong to Christ, not ourselves (HC, Q&A 1). The Lord's Day is the day in which Jesus takes us to our Father, places us into His arms, and feeds us with the Holy Spirit's food for our souls, the preaching of the gospel and the sacraments. There is, then, nothing better we can do on the Lord's Day than assemble as a people to worship our covenant God together and receive His official means of grace. As the eloquent Anglican J. C. Ryle said:

> Never be absent from God's house on Sundays, without good reason,—never to miss the Lord's Supper when administered in our own congregation,—never to let our place be empty when means of grace are going on, this is one way to be a growing and prosperous Christian. The very sermon that we needlessly miss, may contain a precious word in season for our souls. The very assembly for prayer and praise from which we stay away, may be the very gathering that would have cheered, and stablished, and quickened our hearts.[17]

## CONCLUSION

The Regulative Principle of Worship is what makes Reformed churches so different in form and substance from the mass of contemporary churches across the land today. Any given church in your community will say that its worship is biblical, but the question is whether this is truly the case. What stands out today in most contemporary Christian worship? Rock bands, "relevant sermons" (i.e., things *you* want to hear), dramas, skits, entertaining speakers, and the list goes on. Lost in all this is what God requires. May God cause us to rediscover His Word to reform our worship as in the days of King Josiah (2 Kings 22:8–23:7), and to cry out in the king's words: "For great is the wrath of the LORD that is kindled against us, because our fathers have not obeyed the words of this book, to do according to all that is written concerning us" (2 Kings 22:13).

*Notes*

1  William Temple, *Readings in St. John's Gospel* (London: Macmillan, 1940), 68.

2  Calvin, *Institutes*, 1.2.1.

3  John Calvin, *The Necessity of Reforming the Church* (Audubon, N.J.: Old Paths Publications, 1994), 4.

4  *The Creeds of Christendom*, ed. Philip Schaff, rev. David S. Schaff, 3 vols. (repr.; Grand Rapids: Baker, 1996), 1:358.

5  For two excellent works on worship and its relation to our spiritual life, see Michael S. Horton, *In the Face of God: The Dangers and Delights of Spiritual Intimacy* (Dallas: Word, 1996), and *A Better Way: Rediscovering the Drama of God-Centered Worship* (Grand Rapids: Baker, 2002).

6  The term *Regulative Principle of Worship* was made popular in the 1946 report of the Orthodox Presbyterian Church, "Report of the Committee on Song in Worship Presented to the Thirteenth General Assembly, on the Teaching of Our Standards Respecting the Songs That May Be Sung in the Public Worship of God," *Orthodox Presbyterian Church, Minutes of the General Assembly* (1946), 101–107.

7  On the relationship of the Word to church history in the area of worship, see Daniel R. Hyde, "According to the Custom of the Ancient Church? Examining the Roots of John Calvin's Liturgy," *Puritan Reformed Journal* 1:2 (June 2009): 189–211.

8  John Calvin, *The Epistles of Paul the Apostle to the Galatians, Ephesians, Philippians and Colossians*, trans. T. H. L. Parker, Calvin's New Testament Commentaries, 12

vols. (1965; repr., Grand Rapids: Eerdmans, 1972), 11:343. See also Wilhelmus à
Brakel, *The Christian's Reasonable Service*, trans. Bartel Elshout, 4 vols. (Morgan,
Pa.: Soli Deo Gloria, 1992), 3:114: "This consists in serving God in a manner of
our own devising, or in a manner which has been suggested to us by men—doing
so without concern and investigation as to the manner in which God wants to be
served. We then imagine that God will be pleased with our work as long as we have
a good intent to serve Him by means of that activity. The Lord Jesus rejects this in
Matthew 15:9."

9   Richard Sibbes, "The Returning Backslider: Sermon 11," in *The Works of Richard
Sibbes*, ed. Alexander B. Grosart (1862–64; repr., Edinburgh: Banner of Truth,
2001), 2:386.

10  Michael S. Horton, *Lord and Servant: A Covenant Christology* (Louisville:
Westminster John Knox, 2005), 63.

11  On the Cain and Abel story as it applies to worship, see Horton, *In the Face of God*, 7–9.

12  For a comprehensive exposition and application of Hebrews 11:4, see the excellent
commentary of William Perkins (1558–1602), *A Commentary on Hebrews 11 (1609
Edition)*, ed. John H. Augustine, Pilgrim Classic Commentaries (New York: The
Pilgrim Press, 1991), 14–22.

13  John Calvin, *Commentaries on the Last Four Books of Moses Arranged in the Form
of a Harmony: Vol. 3*, trans. Charles William Bingham (1852–1855; repr., Grand
Rapids: Baker, 1996), 431.

14  Ibid., 432.

15  On the "Puritan" concept of worship, see for example, John Owen, "A Discourse
Concerning Liturgies, and Their Imposition," in *The Works of John Owen*, ed.
William H. Goold, 16 vols. (1850–53; repr., Edinburgh: Banner of Truth, 1965),
15:3–55; cf. Daniel R. Hyde, "For Freedom Christ Has Set Us Free: John Owen's
*A Discourse Concerning Liturgies, And Their Imposition*," *The Confessional
Presbyterian* 4 (2008): 29–42.

16  This section is adapted from Daniel R. Hyde, "A Primer on the Lord's Day," *The
Outlook* 59:7 (July/August 2009): 6–10. For more on the Lord's Day, see Iain D.
Campbell, *On the First Day of the Week: God, the Christian, and the Sabbath*
(Leominster, England: Day One Publications, 2005); James T. Dennison, *The
Market Day of the Soul: The Puritan Doctrine of the Sabbath in England, 1532–1700*
(1983; repr., Reformation Heritage Books. 2008); Joseph A. Pipa, *The Lord's Day*
(Fearn, Scotland: Christian Focus, 1997).

17  J. C. Ryle, *Expository Thoughts on John: Vol. 3* (1873; repr., Edinburgh: Banner of
Truth, 1999), 454–455.

# Nine

# PREACHING & SACRAMENTS: MEANS OF GRACE

> *. . . Since, however, in our ignorance and sloth . . . we need outward helps to beget and increase faith within us, and advance it to its goal, God has also added these aids that he may provide for our weakness. . . . God, therefore, in his wonderful providence accommodating himself to our capacity, has prescribed a way for us, though still far off, to draw near to him.*[1]
>
> —John Calvin

Television, radio, computers, and cell phones are all media of communication. As studies have shown, these media seriously affect how we think, learn, experience the world, and relate to one another.[2] But God has chosen to use different media to communicate. His means (Latin, *media*) of communication are utterly "foolish" to the world because they do not demonstrate great power as the world defines power (1 Cor. 1:18–31). Yet, with God's power behind them, His means of preaching and the sacraments affect people far more deeply and effect His grace in them in a far greater way than any of our technological wonders.

Our final chapter on Reformed distinctives deals with the means by which God communicates His grace to us. As Christians, we need more than verbal communication, that is, God speaking to us and conveying information to us. We also need Him to communicate to us in a more holistic way. We need Him to communicate *Himself* to all our senses and to all the aspects of who we are. A wife needs her husband to do more than give her advice on how to fix her problems; she needs to feel his sympathy, his understanding, and his love. So it is with us as the bride of Christ.

In previous chapters, we have covered the authority of God's Word, His saving grace, our justification by faith alone, the Christian life of sanctification, the marks of a true church, and worship that is according to the Word. But these beliefs are relevant only if we can truly come into contact with the God who created the universe, sustains it by His providential care, and redeems "for himself a people for his own possession" (Titus 2:14). All the doctrines above, no matter how true they are, are meaningless to you and me as impersonal principles if we do not have a personal relationship with God the Father through Jesus Christ in the power of the Holy Spirit.

All of these Reformed principles are important because sinners gather together week by week in the belief that God meets with them. We meet with Him because His authoritative Word calls us to do so. He commands us to meet with Him in worship on His terms and promises to be among His people when they assemble as a congregation that displays the three marks of a church. Yet we cannot see, touch, or hear Him. How, then, do we have an experiential relationship with this God and receive His grace?

The Reformers were clear in teaching that God accomplishes this through His "means of grace." God the Holy Spirit uses these to communicate the holistic presence of God's grace to us. These means are the Word and sacraments:[3]

**Since, then, we are made partakers of Christ and all his benefits by faith only, whence comes this faith?**

The Holy Ghost works it in our hearts by the preaching of the holy Gospel, and confirms it by the use of the holy Sacraments. (HC, Q&A 65)

In this chapter, therefore, I want to briefly explore these two means of grace that we might better understand how preaching and the sacraments operate in the church and come to value them as the priceless media of grace that bring us into vital communion with our Lord.

## THE PREACHING OF THE GOSPEL

The chief and primary means by which the Holy Spirit communicates the grace of God to us is the preaching of the gospel. It is by preaching, first of all, that He creates faith within us. As Paul says, "Faith comes from hearing, and hearing through the word of Christ" (Rom. 10:17). The "word of Christ," which is the preached word of the gospel, is the means through which the Holy Spirit gives faith to faithless sinners. But do not think preaching is only for unbelievers. It is also the means whereby the Lord gives His people faith that they might continually trust Him and His promises. This is why we call preaching the primary means of grace.

The Belgic Confession says the Holy Spirit "kindleth" faith in us (Art. 22), and that it is "wrought in man by the hearing of the Word of God and the operation of the Holy Ghost" (Art. 24). When the powerful Holy Spirit accompanies the preached gospel, He gives new life and faith to those who hear. The Canons of Dort speak of the preaching of the gospel, saying, "What, therefore, neither the light of nature nor the law could do, that God performs by the operation of His Holy Spirit through the word or ministry of reconciliation" (3/4.6). In other words, preaching does what neither our own abilities nor even the law of God can do. The Spirit's work through preaching is explained in more detail when the Canons go on to speak of His power and internal work within us:

> . . . he not only causes the gospel to be externally preached to them, and powerfully illuminates their minds by His Holy Spirit, that they may rightly understand and discern the things of the Spirit of God, but by the efficacy of the same regenerating Spirit he pervades the inmost recesses of the man; he opens the closed and softens the hardened heart, and circumcises that which was uncircumcised; infuses new qualities into the will, which, though heretofore dead, he quickens; from being evil, disobedient, and refractory, he renders it good, obedient, and pliable; actuates and strengthens it, that like a good tree, it may bring forth the fruits of good actions. (3/4.11)

All of this tells us that in the preaching ministry of any church, Jesus Christ must be the subject matter, from the beginning of the Bible in Genesis to its end in Revelation. Why would I say this? Simply put, not only did Jesus teach His disciples that all the Old Testament Scriptures were about Him (Luke 24:25–27, 44–47; John 5:39), but the apostle Paul spoke of his own preaching ministry among the Corinthians, saying, "we preach Christ crucified" (1 Cor. 1:23).

Another vital aspect of biblical preaching is that we know that not all who sit and hear the good news about Jesus proclaimed actually believe it. As Jesus taught in the parable of the sower (Matt. 13:1–9, 18–23), preaching is like spreading seed. Some seeds fall along the path and birds eat them; some seeds fall on rocky ground, where they immediately spring up only to be scorched by the sun; some seeds fall among thorns and are choked off; while other seeds fall on good soil and produce grain. For this reason, the preacher must be realistic about the types of people in the congregation. The church is a covenant community, meaning it belongs to Jesus Christ. Yet within the covenant people there are sincere believers as well as hypocrites. Also, unbelieving people from the world are (or at least should be) in our worship services (Zech. 8:20–23; 1 Cor. 14:20–25).

For this reason, Reformed preaching emphasizes both the law and the gospel. The law does two things. First, it humbles the believer, constantly exposing his sins before the Lord. Second, the law either causes the unbeliever to see his or her sin (if it is accompanied by the work of the Spirit) or hardens the unbeliever who will not acknowledge his or her sin. The gospel does two things as well.

First, it comforts and confirms the believer in his or her salvation, constantly reminding of what Jesus did for him or her. Second, the gospel sincerely offers the unbeliever the only means of escaping eternal judgment for his or her sin. As the Canons of Dort say:

> Moreover the promise of the gospel is, that whosoever believes in Christ crucified shall not perish, but have eternal life. This promise, together with the command to repent and believe, ought to be declared and published to all nations, and to all persons promiscuously and without distinction, to whom God out of his good pleasure sends the gospel. (2.5)

> As many as are called by the gospel are unfeignedly [sincerely] called; for God hath most earnestly and truly declared in his Word what will be acceptable to him, namely, that all who are called should comply with the invitation. He, moreover, seriously promises eternal life and rest to as many as shall come to him, and believe on him. (3/4.8)

Whether the prophets preached to the covenant people of Israel or the nations; whether Jesus Christ preached to Israel, His disciples, or the Gentiles; and whether Paul preached to unbelieving Jews and Gentiles or the various congregations of the New Testament, all these preachers always emphasized the need for genuine repentance and true faith. They did this in such a way that believers were constantly comforted while unbelievers were unceasingly discomforted. With this in mind, we can understand the meaning of the Heidelberg Catechism when it contrasts the idols of the Roman

Catholic Church, such as statues, stained-glass windows, and images, with the "lively preaching of [His] Word" (HC, Q&A 98).[4]

## THE SACRAMENTS

The Holy Spirit confirms the faith He creates in His people by the two sacraments of baptism and the Lord's Supper. This is why we speak of them as signs and seals. As signs, they are visible means that point us to the reality that we are washed from sin by the blood and Spirit of Christ (HC, Q&A 69–70). As seals, they are means that the Holy Spirit uses to confirm our faith.

In contrast with the Roman Catholic Church, which sees five additional sacraments—confirmation, penance, marriage, ordination, and last rites—Reformed churches believe Christ instituted just two sacraments. While Rome believes its seven sacraments are works by which people cooperate with God to receive His grace, we believe these are means by which God works to sanctify us and strengthen our faith as we live as pilgrims in this life. In other words, like preaching, the sacraments are media by which God communicates His grace to us in a more tangible way:

> We believe that our gracious God, on account of our weakness and infirmities, hath ordained the Sacraments for us, thereby to seal unto us his promises, and to be pledges of the good will and grace of God towards us, and also to nourish and strengthen our faith, which he hath joined to the word of the gospel, the better to present to our senses, both that which he signifies to us by his Word, and that which he works inwardly in our hearts, thereby assuring

and confirming in us the salvation which he imparts to us.
(BC, Art. 34)

## *Baptism*

Baptism is a means of grace because it is the sacrament of initiation into the covenant community. By it, "we are received into the Church of God, and separated from all other people and strange religions, that we may wholly belong to him whose ensign and banner we bear" (BC, Art. 34). Whether it is administered in childhood or adulthood, baptism places us in the covenant community, as we say, giving us the privileges and benefits of attending public worship, hearing the Word preached, participating in prayer and catechism, and living among the people of God.[5]

Baptism is a means of grace because for those who embrace what baptism signifies—the washing away of our sins by the blood and Spirit of Christ—their faith is constantly assured. This means baptism has lifelong benefits for believers: "Neither doth this Baptism only avail us at the time when the water is poured upon us and received by us, but also through the whole course of our life" (BC, Art. 34). We are strengthened by baptism as we look back to it throughout our lives, "improving" (that is, appropriating) the benefits of Christ for ourselves (WLC, Q&A 167).

What this means practically in a Reformed church is that every time the faithful witness a baptism, either that of an infant or of a new convert, they recall their own baptisms. When they hear the question asked, "Do you openly accept God's covenant promise, which has been signified and sealed unto you in your baptism,"[6] they respond to it in their hearts, remembering what their baptism signifies: "Do you not know that all of us who have been baptized into

Christ Jesus were baptized into his death? We were buried therefore with him by baptism into death, in order that, just as Christ was raised from the dead by the glory of the Father, we too might walk in newness of life" (Rom. 6:3–4).

One additional practical way in which baptism serves as a means of grace all life long is in helping us overcome sin and doubt. As John Calvin said, "Therefore, as often as we fall away, we ought to recall the memory of our baptism and fortify our mind with it, that we may always be sure and confident of the forgiveness of sins."[7]

### The Lord's Supper

While baptism initiates us into the covenant community, the Lord's Supper is the sacrament of nutrition, feeding us with the body and blood of Christ unto everlasting life as our "spiritual nourishment" (WCF, 29.1). Jesus called His disciples to "take [and] eat" the bread and to "drink" of the cup of wine, as they were the visible means of participating in His death "for the forgiveness of sins" (Matt. 26:26, 27, 28). In John's Gospel, we read Jesus' bread of life discourse, in which He explained the significance of His multiplication of bread for the five thousand in terms of our "eating":

> I am the bread of life; whoever comes to me shall not hunger, and whoever believes in me shall never thirst. . . . Truly, truly, I say to you, whoever believes has eternal life. I am the bread of life. Your fathers ate the manna in the wilderness, and they died. This is the bread that comes down from heaven, so that one may eat of it and not die. I am the living bread that came down from heaven. If anyone eats of this bread, he will live forever. And the bread that I will give

for the life of the world is my flesh. . . . Truly, truly, I say to you, unless you eat the flesh of the Son of Man and drink his blood, you have no life in you. Whoever feeds on my flesh and drinks my blood has eternal life, and I will raise him up on the last day. For my flesh is true food, and my blood is true drink. Whoever feeds on my flesh and drinks my blood abides in me, and I in him. As the living Father sent me, and I live because of the Father, so whoever feeds on me, he also will live because of me. This is the bread that came down from heaven, not like the bread the fathers ate and died. Whoever feeds on this bread will live forever." (John 6:35, 47–51, 53–58)

Christ is the true food and true drink of our souls, and we partake of Him by faith through the sacrament of the Lord's Supper. Just as we believe in Christ through the preached Word for our justification, so we believe in Christ through the visible Word of the Lord's Supper for our nutrition.

For this reason, the historical Reformed liturgies of the Lord's Supper call us to feed upon Christ by faith. For example:

That we, then, may be nourished with Christ, the true heavenly bread, let us not cling with our hearts unto the external bread and wine but lift them up on high in heaven, where Jesus Christ is, our Advocate, at the right hand of His heavenly Father, whither also the articles of our Christian faith direct us; not doubting that we shall be nourished and refreshed in our souls, with His body and blood, through the working of the Holy Spirit, as truly as we receive the holy bread and drink in remembrance of Him.[8]

Another of these liturgies, the *Book of Common Prayer*, has these words for those who partake of the Lord's Supper as they take and eat of the bread and drink of the wine:

The Body of our Lord Jesus Christ, which was given for thee, preserve thy body and soul unto everlasting life. Take and eat this in remembrance that Christ died for thee, and feed on him in thy heart by faith with thanksgiving.

The Blood of our Lord Jesus Christ, which was shed for thee, preserve thy body and soul unto everlasting life. Drink this in remembrance that Christ's Blood was shed for thee, and be thankful.[9]

## CONCLUSION

By the means of the preached Word and the sacraments of baptism and the Lord's Supper, our gracious God meets with us in public worship. By these means, God the Father stoops down to our level as little children in order to communicate to us as well as to bring us into intimate fellowship with Himself. Although these means are not outwardly flashy, exciting, or even seemingly powerful to accomplish what we say they do, they are God's chosen means to sustain His weary pilgrims in the wilderness and to strengthen their faith.

*Notes*

1 Calvin, *Institutes*, 4.1.1.

2 Neil Postman, *Amusing Ourselves to Death: Public Discourse in the Age of Show Business* (New York: Penguin, 1985).

3 For a brief introduction to the Reformed theology of the Word and sacraments as *God's* media in contrast with *man's* media, see Daniel R. Hyde, *In Living Color: Images of Christ and the Means of Grace* (Grandville, Mich.: Reformed Fellowship, 2009).

4 On the doctrine of preaching in the catechism, see Daniel R. Hyde, "The Principle and Practice of Preaching in the Heidelberg Catechism," *Puritan Reformed Journal* 1:1 (January 2009): 97–117.

5 For an explanation of infant baptism, see Daniel R. Hyde, *Jesus Loves the Little Children: Why We Baptize Children* (Grandville, Mich.: Reformed Fellowship, 2006), 55–63.

6 "Public Profession of Faith: Form Number 1," in *Psalter Hymnal* (Grand Rapids: Christian Reformed Church, 1976), 132.

7 Calvin, *Institutes*, 4.15.3.

8 "Celebration of the Lord's Supper: Form Number 1," in *Psalter Hymnal*, 146–147.

9 *The Book of Common Prayer and Administration of the Sacraments and Other Rites and Ceremonies of the Church According to the Use of the Reformed Episcopal Church in North America* (Katy, Texas: The Standing Liturgical Commission of the Reformed Episcopal Church, 2003), 101.

## CONCLUSION

At the beginning of this little book, I invited you to join me in a conversation as you are on your way as a pilgrim into the new world of a Reformed church. No matter what your level of understanding or interest in the beliefs and practices of Reformed churches, I sincerely hope that I have given you some things to think about and that you have been stimulated in your heart and mind. Since a book really is a one-way conversation, though, I heartily encourage you to do the following as a means of following up on what you have read here:

• Begin a real conversation by seeking out a Reformed pastor or friend where you live.

• If you need help doing this, one place to start is the Web site of the North American Presbyterian and Reformed Council (NAPARC), which is a group of confessional and conservative Reformed churches in North America (http://naparc.org). Links there will take you to the home pages of various Reformed denominations in the United States. From those pages, you can locate individual congregations.

• If all else fails, you may contact me with your questions and/or to find a Reformed church in your area (www.oceansideurc.org).

# QUESTIONS & ANSWERS

I do not doubt you have many remaining questions about the beliefs and practices of Reformed churches. In this appendix, I will try to answer some of the most common and not-so-common questions that newcomers to my church have asked me over the years.

### Q. Are you Roman Catholic?

A. No, Reformed churches are not Roman Catholic. As Protestants, we have taken our stand against the false teachings of Rome, as chapters one and two demonstrate. In fact, the authors of the historical Reformed confessions were clear on this, distancing themselves from the Roman Catholic Church by calling her "the false Church" (BC, Art. 29) and calling the pope "that Antichrist, that man of sin and son of perdition, that exalteth himself in the Church against the Church, and all that is called God" (WCF, 25.6, original).

When our forefathers said their churches were *Reformed*, they used a code word by which they said they believed themselves to be Christian churches in the historical *catholic* (small "c," meaning "universal") tradition. The great English Puritan William Perkins even wrote a treatise titled *A Reformed Catholic*, showing that Reformed churches are true catholic Christian churches, not *Roman* Catholic churches.

## Q. Are you fundamentalists?

A. No. Fundamentalism originated as a laudable effort in the early twentieth century to promote fundamental points of historical Christian doctrine that Protestant liberalism rejected, such as the inspiration of the Scriptures, the virgin birth of Christ, His substitutionary death, His resurrection, and His second coming. On these fundamental points of doctrine, all true churches agree.

Fundamentalism in modern thought, however, is more about churches aligning with conservative American politics and even imposing an ideology of "Christian America" on our society. It has come to be associated with insistence on what Christians must not do, such as drink alcohol, and what Christians must believe, such as premillennial eschatology.

## Q. Are you evangelicals?

A. Not in the sense in which the word is used today. Someone has said that an evangelical in our day is one who has had some sort of religious experience with God and who likes Billy Graham. Seriously, though, the word *evangelical* comes from the Greek word for "gospel." The early Reformers called themselves evangelicals because they believed and preached the gospel of Jesus Christ's free grace against the works-oriented salvation of the Roman Catholic Church. Unfortunately, this perfectly good and biblical word has been taken over to mean something it never meant in Scripture or in the history of the Protestant Reformation. In sum, we are not evangelicals according to the modern use of that term, but we are in its historical use.[1]

### Q. Why is your worship so boring, cold, and serious?

A. If a church must have a rock-style band, stage lighting, and tens of thousands of dollars' worth of musical equipment in order for its worship to be considered interesting, exciting, vibrant, and lively, then yes, Reformed churches that do not have all that may sound boring and cold to contemporary ears. This only solidifies the opinion of many Reformed leaders today about the sad state of affairs in modern churches, which have looked more to culture for their paradigm of what constitutes "good" worship than to the Word of God.

As Reformed churches, we believe that interesting, exciting, vibrant, and lively worship occurs every time the gospel of our Lord Jesus Christ is preached purely and the sacraments of baptism and the Lord's Supper are administered according to Christ's institution. We believe that when these things happen, worship is truly "led by the Holy Spirit," Christ-exalting, and edifying to all those who participate by faith.

### Q. Why do Reformed churches sing psalms? They are so boring and irrelevant.

A. Historically speaking, Reformed churches have been distinguished from Roman Catholic and Lutheran churches because they are psalm-singing churches. Whether a Reformed church continues to sing psalms exclusively or sings mostly hymns or contemporary songs with a psalm sung occasionally, there are several good reasons for singing them.

First, we sing psalms because they are biblical; therefore, they transcend all cultures and are edifying to all the people of God. This is why Paul says, "Let the word of Christ dwell in you richly, teaching and admonishing one another in all wisdom, singing psalms and hymns and spiritual songs, with thankfulness in your hearts to God" (Col. 3:16). Although the tunes for these psalms may be boring (and we can change them), the words are neither boring nor irrelevant, for they are God's Word.

Second, we sing psalms because they fully express the range of emotions we as humans and as Christians experience. In his preface to his *Commentary on the Book of Psalms*, John Calvin spoke of these emotions when he said:

> I have been accustomed to call this book [Psalms], I think not inappropriately, *The Anatomy of all the Parts of the Soul* . . . there is not an emotion of which any one can be conscious that is not here represented as in a mirror. Or rather, the Holy Spirit has here drawn . . . all the griefs, sorrows, fears, doubts, hopes, cares, perplexities, in short, all the distracting emotions with which the minds of men are wont to be agitated. The other parts of Scripture contain the commandments which God enjoined his servants to announce to us. But here the prophets themselves, seeing they are exhibited to us as speaking to God, and laying open all their inmost thoughts and affections, call, or rather draw, each of us to the examination of himself in particular, in order that none of the many infirmities to which we are subject, and of the many vices with which we abound, may remain concealed. It is certainly a rare and singular advantage, when all lurking places are discovered, and the heart

is brought into the light, purged from that most baneful infection, hypocrisy.[2]

Third, we sing psalms because they speak of Jesus Christ (Luke 24:44). Through the psalms, we sing of His deity (Ps. 45:6–7), His birth (Pss. 8:5; 40:7–9), His office of Prophet (Ps. 22:22), His office of Priest (Ps. 110:4), His office of King (Ps. 110:1), His trial (Ps. 35:11–12), His rejection (Ps. 118:22–23), His crucifixion (Pss. 22:1–21; 69:1–4), His burial and resurrection (Ps. 16:8–11), His ascension (Pss. 47:5; 68:18), and His second coming (Ps. 98:7–9).

### Q. Do you care about evangelism?

A. Yes. Like many of these questions, this one assumes the modern American evangelical premise that true "evangelism" means supporting Billy Graham crusades or the Harvest Crusade, or having an altar call at the end of an "evangelistic" service—of course, with the lights dimmed, every eye closed, and every head bowed. Those new to Reformed church faith and life need to learn of the evangelistic and church-planting fervor of our Reformed forefathers, including Calvin himself.[3] It was the example of Calvin's Geneva that led to the modern missions movement, under the leadership of pioneers such as David Brainerd (1718–1747) among the American Indians, William Carey (1761–1834) in India, Henry Martyn (1781–1812) in India and Persia, Adoniram Judson (1788–1850) in Burma, John Paton (1824–1907) in the New Hebrides, and Jonathan Goforth (1859–1936) in China. As Carey said after chronicling the state of the nations of the world in his day, "All these things are loud calls to Christians, and especially to ministers, to exert themselves to the utmost in their several spheres of action, and to try to enlarge them as much as possible."[4]

Reformed churches believe there is a biblical distinction between evangelism and witness. Evangelism is properly the public preaching of the gospel. For example, Paul speaks of this in Romans 10, where he explains that people come to call upon the name of the Lord through sent preachers who preach Christ, and that faith is given to those who hear to embrace Christ (Rom. 10:17). This is also what Paul told Timothy, who was a "minister" of the Word (1 Tim. 4:6; NIV), when he said, "Do the work of an evangelist, fulfill your ministry" (2 Tim. 4:5). On the other hand, the biblical idea of witness is what all believers engage in with their lips and lives. This is what Jesus meant when He told His disciples to be salt and light (Matt. 5:13–16) and what Peter meant when he told the early Christians in Asia Minor that one Christian virtue was "always being prepared to make a defense to anyone who asks you for a reason for the hope that is in you" (1 Peter 3:15).

This crucial distinction actually frees ministers and missionaries to fulfill their callings as preachers and evangelists, while freeing the people of God to do what they are called to do: bear witness to the Christian faith that is revealed in Scripture as well as their own personal faith, and to back it up with prayer and holy lives.

### Q. Are you anti-Semitic?

A. No. Because most modern fundamentalist and evangelical churches hold to a view of the end of time in which the nation of Israel plays a central part, those churches that do not hold to this interpretation are often called anti-Semitic. Saying we are not anti-Semitic is no theory, though, but a practical truth. Go to a Reformed church that has roots in the Dutch Reformed Church and speak with older members who immigrated to America. Ask them about hiding Jews from the Nazis. Then you will have your answer. Reformed churches recognize that the Scriptures call us to pray "for all people" (1 Tim. 2:1), whether they are Jewish or Gentile.

## Q. Why are you so theological? You should be more practical. Christianity is all about actions such as feeding the homeless.

A. This question assumes a dichotomy, which the modern church has brought in from our culture, in which theory and practice are divorced.[5] Who needs to learn math when we have computers, right? As Christians, our heavenly Father has rescued us from the bondage of such a mind-set, calling us to love Him with all that we are, our minds (Matt. 22:37; Rom. 12:2) as well as our bodies (Rom. 12:1). This means that what we believe about God actually has practical effects on how we live our lives before Him in the world He has made.

The question for us really is this: Why should we actually feed the homeless? I ask this because the premise that Christianity is about doing things and not about believing things is itself a theological belief. Anything we say in response to this question is theology. We seek to have the mind of Christ (Phil. 2:5) so that we will be empowered biblically to live for the Lord.

So why should we care about feeding the homeless? We should care because it is a way of showing Christ's concern for them and, Lord willing, sharing the gospel of eternal life with them. God cares for the outcast and, in fact, became an outcast in Jesus Christ.

## Q. Why do you put so much emphasis on John Calvin and Martin Luther, for example? Isn't Christianity all about Jesus Christ?

A. Yes, our faith is all about God. One of the slogans that came out of the Reformation is *soli Deo gloria*, or "To God alone be glory."

Because of this, Calvin was buried in an unmarked grave and Luther warned his people never to follow him. We talk about them because, in the providence of God, these men were gifted with the talents and abilities to build up the church in its faith at a time when these gifts were most needed. Our focus is not on the men themselves, but on what they taught so clearly about our faith and focus on Jesus Christ. As I said earlier, the churches of the Reformation were called "Calvinist" and "Lutheran" only by their enemies.

### Q. Why do you seem so strict and "legalistic"?

A. In a culture in which anything goes, in which every opinion means just as much as any other, Reformed churches may seem "legalistic." However, it is important to understand this word.

Legalism is properly a belief that our works and cooperation play a part in our salvation, however small that part may be. It is not legalism when we as Reformed churches say that God calls us to worship Him on Sunday instead of providing a convenient Saturday night service so people can do what they want on Sunday. This is seeking to follow Scripture and not to follow the rules of the world. In fact, it may be that Reformed churches are not legalistic but that other churches are libertine, licentious, or antinomian.

### Q. Is there a Reformed view of creation?

A. I wouldn't say there is a distinctly "Reformed" view of creation, since what we confess to believe about creation is historical Christian doctrine (BC, Art. 12; HC, Q&A 26): God created heaven, earth, and all creatures through His Word (Heb. 1:2) and Spirit (Gen. 1:2), He did so out of nothing (Gen. 1:1; Heb. 11:3), and He did so "in the space of six days" (Gen. 1:1–2:3; WCF, 1.1). All of His creative work was for His own glory (Rom. 11:33–36). These truths were embraced by the church for most of its history.

Of course, the doctrine of the goodness of creation (Gen. 1:31) has a particular emphasis in the Reformed faith. For example, because of God's creation of all things, we believe in the nobility of the Christian's vocation, whether it be in the area of sanitation, public service, homemaking, or pastoring. Our understanding of creation also affects how we view the way in which God meets and speaks with us through His Word, since it is written on ordinary paper with ordinary ink and it is preached by the voice of an ordinary man, and how He communicates His grace to us through water, bread, and wine—elements of this created realm. In fact, our doctrine of creation also affects our doctrine of the new heavens and the new earth, which we believe will be the existing heavens and earth resurrected, just as Jesus was, to their original intent.

## Q. *What do Reformed churches believe about the Holy Spirit?*

A. Along with all true churches in all times and places, we confess that the Holy Spirit is a person like the Father and the Son, co-eternal God with them (HC, Q&A 53; BC, Art. 11). As God, His role in our salvation is primarily that of sanctifying and setting us apart for the Lord's service. He gives us new birth (John 3:1–8), He gives us faith to embrace Jesus Christ (Eph. 2:8), He strengthens us through the preaching of the Word and the sacraments, He lifts our hearts to heaven in worship, and He empowers us to live for the glory of God (Gal. 5:16–26).[6]

## Q. *What do Reformed churches believe about "the end times"?*

A. We confess with the historical Christian church that our "blessed hope" is the "appearing of the glory of our great God and Savior Jesus

Christ" (Titus 2:13). When He comes again "to judge the living and the dead" (Apostles' Creed), He will raise all men and judge all men by sending His enemies into eternal punishment and His friends into eternal blessedness in the new heavens and new earth (Rev. 21–22). All of this is described in the Belgic Confession, Article 37, which ends: "Therefore we expect that great day with a most ardent desire, to the end that we may fully enjoy the promises of God in Christ Jesus our Lord. Amen."[7]

## Notes

1   See R. Scott Clark, *Recovering the Reformed Confession: Our Theology, Piety, and Practice* (Phillipsburg, N.J.: P&R, 2008).

2   John Calvin, *Commentary on the Book of Psalms: Vol. One*, trans. James Anderson, Calvin's Commentaries, 22 vols. (repr.; Grand Rapids: Baker, 1996), 4:xxxvi–xxxvii.

3   On the mission emphasis of John Calvin, see R. Pierce Beaver, "The Genevan Mission to Brazil," in *The Heritage of John Calvin*, ed. John Bratt (Grand Rapids: Eerdmans, 1973), 55–73, and Joel R. Beeke, "Calvin's Evangelism," in *Living for God's Glory: An Introduction to Calvinism* (Orlando, Fla.: Reformation Trust, 2008), 275–288.

4   William Carey, *An Enquiry into the Obligations of Christians to Use Means for the Conversion of the Heathens* (Leicester, England: Ann Ireland, 1792), as found at http://www.gutenberg.org/catalog/world/readfile?fk_files=51264&pageno=21 (accessed April 2, 2009).

5   On this false dichotomy, see J. Gresham Machen, *Christianity and Liberalism* (Grand Rapids: Eerdmans, 1923).

6   For a treatment of the comprehensiveness of the Holy Spirit in Reformed theology, see Daniel R. Hyde, "The Holy Spirit in the Heidelberg Catechism," *Mid-America Journal of Theology* 17 (2006): 211–37.

7   For Reformed treatments of eschatology, see Kim Riddlebarger, *A Case for Amillennialism* (Grand Rapids: Baker, 2003), and Cornelis P. Venema, *The Promise of the Future* (Edinburgh: Banner of Truth, 2000).

# A BASIC BIBLIOGRAPHY

King Solomon once said to his son, "Of making many books there is no end" (Eccl. 12:12). If this was true in the ninth century before Christ, how much more true is it today? There are many books to choose from in the marketplace, so what follows is an extremely brief list of those books that will help you on your way as you explore the theology, history, liturgy, and community of a Reformed church.

## THEOLOGY

As you explore Reformed Christianity's beliefs, the most basic way to start is by obtaining and reading the Reformed confessions themselves, mentioned in chapter one. The following is a basic list of expositions of what these confessions teach.

### *General*

• W. Robert Godfrey, *An Unexpected Journey: Discovering Reformed Christianity* (P&R, 2004). Godfrey is president of Westminster Seminary California, a Reformed seminary in Southern

California. This book is his autobiography, in which he weaves a basic explanation of Reformed beliefs.

• Michael Horton, *Putting Amazing Back into Grace* (Baker, 2002). Horton's book delves into our theology in a biblical and historical way. It is a modern-day classic that has changed countless lives.

• R. C. Sproul, *What Is Reformed Theology? Understanding the Basics* (Baker, 2005). Sproul's book is another excellent resource that introduces the theology of the Reformation.

• John Calvin, *Institutes of the Christian Religion* (The Westminster Press, 1960). Calvin's masterwork is the classic explanation of what the Reformed churches are all about. Finished in 1559, this work is saturated with Scripture and helpfully interacts with all the questions of theology, as well as why Reformed churches are catholic churches, just not *Roman* Catholic churches.

### Covenant

• Michael Horton, *God of Promise: Introducing Covenant Theology* (Baker, 2006). Since Reformed theology is so much more than the doctrine of predestination, it is essential that you understand how Reformed Christians read Scripture through the lens that God has given us: His covenant relationship with us. A great place to start is with Horton. He deprograms Christians and non-Christians alike from all the end-times hysteria of modern-day "dispensationalism" (a theological belief system in which Israel and the church are divided into two peoples with two different redemptive plans).

## God

Three books about our doctrine of God stand out as essential reading for those new to Reformed churches. These books are not merely academic, dry treatises about God, but devotional books that lead us to the throne of grace.

• J. I. Packer, *Knowing God* (InterVarsity Press, 1993). Packer's modern-day classic masterfully exposits the attributes of our triune God and brings us into closer communion with Him.

• R. C. Sproul, *The Holiness of God* (Tyndale House, 2000). Sproul's most famous book recounts the teaching in Scripture about the "holy, holy, holy" God of Isaiah 6, which changed his life.

• R. C. Sproul, *Chosen by God* (Tyndale House, 1994). This lesser-known book by Sproul expresses the essential Reformed belief that God is sovereign and has elected a people for Himself from eternity.

## Jesus Christ

• Daniel R. Hyde, *God With Us: Knowing the Mystery of Who Jesus Is* (Reformation Heritage Books, 2007). This is a basic exposition of the incarnation of the Son of God as one person with two natures, and how that affects the Christian life.

• R. C. Sproul, *The Glory of Christ* (P&R, 2003). This book is another excellent introductory work on the wonder of our Savior.

## The Holy Spirit

• Sinclair Ferguson, *The Holy Spirit* (InterVarsity Press, 1997). This is a phenomenal book on the Holy Spirit, incorporating the best of the Reformed and Puritan tradition.

• R. C. Sproul, *The Mystery of the Holy Spirit* (Christian Focus, 2009). This book is a great introduction to the Reformed perspective on the person and work of the Holy Spirit.

### Sacraments

• Daniel R. Hyde, *Jesus Loves the Little Children: Why We Baptize Children* (Reformed Fellowship, 2006). This is a concise, clear, and charitable presentation of the Reformed churches' understanding of infant baptism.

## HISTORY

### The Reformation

It is important to grasp our historical roots and our place in the history of God's dealings with His people.

• W. Robert Godfrey, *Reformation Sketches: Insights into Luther, Calvin, and the Confessions* (P&R, 2003). Someone once said Godfrey makes dead people and old places come alive. In this little book, he does just that.

• Diarmaid MacCulloch, *The Reformation: A History* (Penguin, 2003). This is a fascinating retelling of the background, culture, and religion of the medieval world that led to the Reformation. MacCulloch is critical of the Reformation, but his historical research is compelling.

### Confessions

• Philip Schaff (ed.), *The Creeds of Christendom*, rev. David S. Schaff, 3 vols. (Baker, reprinted 1996). This is a classic repository of the Lutheran, Reformed, and even modern creeds, catechisms, and confessions of faith.

- Daniel R. Hyde, *With Heart and Mouth: An Exposition of the Belgic Confession* (Reformed Fellowship, 2008). This book, the first comprehensive commentary on the Belgic Confession of Faith since 1960, seeks to explain the text and apply it for our time.
- Willem Van't Spijker (ed.), *The Church's Book of Comfort* (Reformation Heritage Books, 2009). This book contains a popular introduction to the history, personalities, and theology of the Heidelberg Catechism by several pastors and professors in the Netherlands.
- Peter Y. De Jong (ed.), *Crisis in the Reformed Churches: Essays in Commemoration of the Great Synod of Dort, 1618–19* (Reformed Fellowship, 2008). This classic book looks at the history, theology, and people behind the Synod of Dort in the Netherlands.
- R. C. Sproul, *Truths We Confess: A Layman's Guide to the Westminster Confession of Faith*, 3 vols. (P&R, 2006–2007). The theology of the Westminster Confession is unfolded by one of the greatest contemporary Reformed theologians.

## LITURGY

Theology that does not lead to doxology (praise of God) is not worthy of the name. This is why Reformed Christians have been so zealous to worship God. We have been diligent to understand and communicate what Christian worship should look like, why we use a liturgy, and why our focus in worship is on preaching and sacraments, not on just being "led by the Spirit."

- Daniel R. Hyde, *What to Expect in Reformed Worship: A Visitor's Guide* (Wipf & Stock, 2007). This is a small booklet for church literature racks that gives an overview of Reformed worship for those who visit a Reformed church for the first time.

• Michael Horton, *A Better Way: Rediscovering the Drama of God-Centered Worship* (Baker, 2002). Horton explores the principles and practice of Reformed liturgy in a comprehensive way that will engage your heart and mind on this vital topic.

• *Psalter Hymnal* (Christian Reformed Church, 1976).

• *Trinity Hymnal* (rev. ed.; Great Commission Publications, 1990).

• *Trinity Psalter* (Crown & Covenant Publications, 1994).

## COMMUNITY

Theology leads to liturgy, which leads to our common life as a community of saints. Several books will help you deal with various practical issues from a Reformed point of view.

### *Evangelism*

Do Calvinists believe in evangelism? The two best books on a Reformed approach to evangelism are:

• Will Metzger, *Tell the Truth: The Whole Gospel to the Whole Person by Whole People* (InterVarsity Press, 2002).

• R. B. Kuiper, *God-Centered Evangelism* (Banner of Truth, 1966).

### *Hospitality*

• Mary Beeke with Joel Beeke, *The Law of Kindness: Serving with Heart and Hands* (Reformation Heritage Books, 2007).

• Marva J. Dawn, *Truly the Community: Romans 12 and How to Be the Church* (Eerdmans, 1992).

## Suffering

How do we deal with suffering, the painful part of our sanctification in this age before Christ returns? On this subject I highly recommend:

- Michael Horton, *Too Good to Be True: Finding Hope in a World of Hype* (Zondervan, 2006).

## Family Catechism

What is the role of parents in bringing their children up in the "discipline and instruction of the Lord" (Eph 6:4)?

- Donald Van Dyken, *Rediscovering Catechism: The Art of Equipping Children* (P&R, 2000). This book is a treasure. It not only explains the biblical and historical roots of parents catechizing (instructing) their children, but also gives practical advice on how to implement catechizing in the home.

Of course, there are many more books under the sun than one can read in a lifetime, but these select few will get you going in your exploration of Reformed Christianity.

# Index 1
# SCRIPTURE REFERENCES

166

## ABOUT THE AUTHOR

Rev. Daniel R. Hyde is the pastor of the Oceanside United Reformed Church in Carlsbad/Oceanside, California, a congregation of the United Reformed Churches in North America (http://urcna.org/).

A native of Long Beach, California, Rev. Hyde was baptized into the Roman Catholic Church. He was converted to Christ at age 17 in a Foursquare Church and encountered the Reformed faith at an Assemblies of God college, where he earned his bachelor's degree in religion.

He earned his master of divinity degree from Westminster Seminary California, where he was mentored by Drs. W. Robert Godfrey, Michael Horton, and R. Scott Clark. He earned his master of theology in Reformation and post-Reformation theology at Puritan Reformed Theological Seminary, where his thesis advisors were Drs. Joel R. Beeke and Derek W. H. Thomas.

Rev. Hyde has written a number of books, including *Jesus Loves the Little Children*, *The Good Confession*, *What to Expect in Reformed Worship*, *God with Us*, *With Heart and Mouth*, and *In Living Color*. He also has written numerous articles and chapters for books.

He lives in Oceanside with his wife and college sweetheart, Karajean, their sons, Cyprian, Caiden, and Daxton, and their dachshund, Xerxes.